The
Well-Watered
Life

TODD L. SHULER

PRAISE FOR
THE WELL-WATERED LIFE

☆☆☆☆☆

"…Practical and Encouraging…"
—*Readers' Favorite* rates *The Well-Watered Life* – 5 out of 5 stars

"If you wonder why your spiritual tank is running on empty or if you are looking
for a glimpse of hope and definite purpose for your life,
this book was written for you. Reading it may be the first step to a more fulfilling
and passionate spiritual journey."
—*Luis Castro,* Certified Coach, Teacher & Speaker for The John Maxwell Team

"I know that everyone who reads this book will be blessed."
—*Yvonne Hurst,* Salvation Army (Retired)

"This book is an indispensable tool for the lay member and leader alike who find
themselves in a desert place. Shuler fascinates his reader with his practical insights
and biblical wisdom. It's a must-read for the person whose life's journey has lost
passion, power, and purpose. The reader will be transformed from wandering in
the desert to having an intimate, fulfilled life in Christ. I highly recommend this
book for those beginning their walk with Christ or those who seek to continue
toward the mature, well-watered life!"
—*Dr. Carlos McCloud,* Theologian

"*The Well-Watered Life* offers practical strategies for new and seasoned Christians to
use in the tough times of their lives. It contains real-world situations reminding us
we are not alone in our life's journey to God's kingdom."
—*Tammy Dye Walls,* Middle School Teacher

"In a culture that has lowered practically all moral and ethical standards over the
course of the past couple of decades, Todd Shuler's *The Well-Watered Life* does an
exceptional job in pointing believers back to the basics of prayer, seeking God, and
listening for His answers. Todd vividly portrays the healthy and dynamic Christian
life as one of intentionality; the reader is brought to the brink of decision as to the
future direction of his life as a follower of Christ."
—*Stan Hutchinson*, Engineer, Financial Counselor and Instructor,
Author of *Financial Peace of Mind from the WORD*

"Great Book! Very Inspirational. A must-read no matter where you are
in your Christian walk."
—*David Williams, Jr.,* Information Technology Security Professional

The Well-Watered Life by Todd Shuler
Published by City of God Publishing
(a division of Crown Global Corporation)
223 Wimbledon Place
Macon, GA 31211

ISBN: 0988958902
ISBN-13: 978-0988958906

For Worldwide Distribution
Printed in the U.S.A.

This book and all other City of God Publishing books are available at Christian bookstores, online retailers and distributors worldwide.

For more information, contact us at (404) 939-0807
Or reach us on the Web:
www.cityofgodpublishing.com

DEDICATION

To the God of Abraham, Isaac, and Jacob...

To the God of my matriarchs—
Ms. Octavia Hill Shuler (1905-2005)
and Ms. Henrietta Ava Lockett (1914-2003)...

To the God of my parents—
Bishop Allen J. Shuler, Sr. and Mrs. Sallie Lockett Shuler...

To the God of my favorite Uncle and Auntie "Lean"—
Mr. Easter "Henry" (1938-1996) and Mrs. Everlean Finney...

To the God of my lovely wife, Evetta...

Evetta and I pray, as imperfect parents showing imperfect love,
that our wonderful children—Trevor, Philip, Lauren and Serina
(our daughter-in-grace) — will also choose to love and follow You
with every fiber of their being.

To the God of my mother-in-law, Dr. Pamela Lewis.

To so many others who have loved, encouraged, and prayed for me
(in spite of myself) down through the years...

Most of all, to my Lord Jesus Christ—My Master, Savior, King, Brother,
and Friend. Thank You for giving Your Life for me
and all those who will read this book, believe in You,
and receive the "Well-Watered Life"—life eternal.
To You be the Glory, Dominion, and Power.
Forever and Amen!

CONTENTS

ACKNOWLEDGMENTS

My heartfelt gratitude and thanks to these wonderful people who helped create The Well-Watered Life. To Mom and Dad, who inspired me to write as a kid after I read copies of their own short stories and poems left around the house.

To my siblings (and their spouses):
Allen Jr. (Constance), Shena (Anthony), Serina, and Dana.

To my "spiritual fathers and mothers" (past and present): Rev. William A. Holt, (deceased), Rev. Amos Kemper III, Mrs. Eva Fulton (deceased), Rev. Francis Marion (deceased), Mrs. Lula Mae Ray (deceased), Mrs. Thelma Burke, Bishop Cephus J. and Mrs. Victoria Hicks (both deceased), Bishop Cornelius and Mrs. Pinkie Demps (both deceased), Mrs. Gwendolyn Adside (deceased), Dr. Stephen Jordan, Rev. Walter and Mrs. Janlynn Fleming, Rev. Odell Barnwell (deceased), Bishop Chandler David Owens (deceased), Deacon and Mrs. Clarence Bloodsaw, Ms. Bernice Hannah (deceased), Rev. Alexander Anderson (deceased), Rev. Evans D. and Mrs. Pearlie Brown, Dr. Gregory Clinton, Dr. Gregory Broughton, Dr. Johann Buis, Dr. Verney Clarke, Dr. Doug Beacham, Mr. Donald Stewart, Rev. Lee Norris, Mr. John and Mrs. Vermell Leslie, Mr. Woody and Mrs. Shigeko Whitley, Bishop Dale Bronner, Dr. Bobby and Mrs. Jean Ross (both deceased), Pastors Steve and Debbie Sawyer, Bishop Samuel and Mrs. Rheba Drye, and Bishop Bo and Mrs. Melissa Turner.

To the Real Life Church of God (Macon, GA) Usher Team: Barry Bacon, Joe Benton, Michael Bledsoe, Steve Brookins, Rick Cheatham, Alan Dumas, Carl Dunson, Eddie Dunson, Jeff Fowler, Jimmy Freeman, Marty Griffin, Robert "Bob" Grizzard, John Manning, Mark Molina, Marvin Wells, and Shane Whittington.
Thanks for allowing me to serve our members, staff, and guests with you at the pleasure of the Lord and our Pastor while being able to praise, worship, and dance together each week on "God's Great Dance Floor."

To the past and present members of
the United States Army Reserve Unit
341st Adjunct General Company, Athens, GA:
I am proud to have served our nation with you both at home and abroad.

To my editors:
Angela Cook, LaConia Dean, Kelley Land, Crystal Pitman,
Carolyn Roark, Evetta Shuler, and June Saunders.

Finally, to the wonderful people who were willing
to volunteer their time to get this book across the finish line:
Pastor Stacey Bass, Matt Blanchard, Renay Bloom, Bettye Burney,
Robin Castro, Angela Cherry, Jake Cox, Tim Culbertson,
Marcy Lewis Ellerbee, Brian Ezeike, Byron Fleming, Anne Gardner,
Randy Groomes, Gwendolyn Harvey, Arnetta Hatten, LaQuonne Holden,
Lynette Howard, Pamela James, Schanea Fleming Kelly, Hope Lattimore,
Stephanie Leggett, Richard Madison, Charlie Merritt, Evette Mills,
Carlos Miro, Rachel Moore, Eddie Murphy, Nwabu Okeiyi,
Michelle Rumph, Darren Short, Karen Star, James Taylor,
Remeka Turk, Andrea Walthour and Heather Wise.

God bless each and every one of you!

FOREWORD

The Well-Watered Life carefully explores our complex relationship to one of life's simplest elements. Todd Shuler's careful study of both the Old and New Testaments reminds us that, while physical water is so precious that wars have been fought over it, having our spiritual thirst assuaged at the Well of Living Water is even more vital.

Throughout the book, he reiterates how many biblical characters had natural and spiritual encounters at wells. He beckons us to peer into and drink deeply from the well of living water. He weaves a beautiful tapestry of meditation on the significance of prayer and obedience to satisfy our thirst for deeper meaning and harmony.

Shuler helps us to understand the passage of generational blessings or curses, which were dependent on the obedience of the patriarchs. He challenges modern-day believers to understand this concept and not to underestimate heartfelt and earnest prayer, coupled with the Holy Spirit's power, to resolve issues in our everyday relationships and experiences.

Shuler's analysis brings biblical concepts alive in a wonderful way using these accessible tools:

- Quotes from seasoned and influential authors
- Poems
- Movies
- Books
- Songs
- Hebrew and Greek definitions
- Personal experiences

He highlights the ways in which Isaac's lifelong obedience to God's will and ways affected many generations centuries later. He symbolically portrays Jacob's well to emphasize how many nations were blessed through the lineage of Abraham, Isaac, and Jacob.

Todd's obedience to natural and spiritual authority is also born out through personal stories that demonstrate how prayerful obedience quite literally wrought a great victory for the preservation of God's Word.

The final chapter of the book reminds us of the ongoing significance of Jacob's well: Jesus' encounter with the Samaritan woman and His revelation of living water.

Oh, that our modern-day families would seize upon the concept of generational blessings! And that we would indeed drink deeply and often from the well of living water, especially in the area of our relationships.

Dr. Samuel Drye and Mrs. Rheba Drye
Founders, Destiny Life Ministries International (DLMI)
Macon, GA

Todd's Gift to You, the Reader:

Download *The Well-Watered Life
Personal Study Guide* (PDF) for FREE at
www.wellwateredlife.com

The Well-Watered Life
Experiencing God's Goodness in the Desert Places of Your Life

1
WHAT MAKES YOU THIRSTY?

Nothing is more breathtaking than experiencing the beauty of God's great outdoors. As magnificent as our manmade structures are, the great outdoors is unrivaled in its expanses, beauty, and sweeping vistas. Snow-capped mountains, rolling plains, crystal-clear water, and sugar-white beaches are indelibly etched in my mind. And who can forget sharing a magical, romantic experience on a silver moonlit night or the golden sun whose rays warm our faces on a chilling winter day?

Yet, despite its wonderment, nature can be challenging. Take, for instance, the summers of the southern United States with their smoldering temperatures above 100 degrees. As the sun's heat beats down on you, your body seeks desperately to cool itself. Beads of perspiration appear, drenching your clothing and quenching your skin.

Internally, something just as dramatic is taking place. You know the symptoms: a dry throat, chapped lips, and the uncontrollable urge to keep swallowing. You are thirsty.

You drop everything you are working on. Nothing else matters. You have to do something fast: anything to quench your tortured thirst.

So what do you reach for? Coca-Cola™? Pepsi™? Gatorade™? Sweet tea? Lemonade? As wonderful as these beverages are, nothing stops thirst dead in its tracks like a tall glass of refreshing, ice-cold water. Cold water soothes the palate and the soul. Scientists refer to water as a base substance, which simply means that when the water reaches your acid-filled stomach, it calms and temporarily relaxes it. It is the world's first and foremost solvent.

Water is essential to the human body. You can last several weeks without food, but you can only last about one week without water. Your body, like our world, is seventy percent water. It is one of the great wonders of the world. It is a human's main cleansing agent: we use it to cook, wash, and bathe. We swim in water. It is essential for all life, including the lives of the plants we eat that support the animals we consume. Water is life.

Water is so important that states like Florida, Georgia, and Tennessee fight in court over the use of the Chattahoochee River. In January 2014, authorities in West Virginia scrambled to contain a chemical spill in the Elk River by a private firm which left over 300,000 desperate residents without water to drink or bathe for a week. Nations divided by rivers fight over water rights. I believe we will see a time in the near future when water will become even more expensive than oil.

Water was so precious in biblical times, especially in the desert lands of the Middle East where biblical stories take place, that plugging up or even using someone else's well was considered an act of war. There is an unforgettable scene in the movie *Lawrence of Arabia* when the use of a desert well resulted in murder. In this moving film, T. E. Lawrence (Peter O'Toole) and his Arab guide, all hot and dusty from the wind and sands, stop at a well—just a hole in the desert with short, mounded walls of sand. In the glaring sunlight, the two haul up a rubber bucket from the well and drink, and then a dark figure appears mysteriously on the horizon. This figure, Sherif Ali (played by Omar Sharif), mercilessly shoots the guide dead in cold blood. When Lawrence raises moral objections to the murder of his guide, Ali shrugs, as if he felt justified. Taking water from another tribe's well is an act of war and is answered by violence. It is simply the way of the desert.

If water could inspire murder in the twentieth century (and still today), you can imagine how precious it was in biblical times. A well was an instrument of survival in the desert and an appropriate symbol for life. In the Bible, wells and water are symbols of both physical and spiritual life.

Wells figured often in the life of Isaac, whose endeavors are an inspiration for this book. Isaac's wife, Rebekah, was found for him when his servant met her at a well. In seeking a wife for his master, Isaac, the man had decided that the right woman would offer him water for himself and for his camels. It would be a sign from God as well as a demonstration that she was generous and kind.

Later, Isaac had to revisit the wells his father Abraham dug and dig them again. (We will go into these stories and their analysis of life lessons for us in future chapters.) Isaac also had a series of interactions with various Philistine herdsmen that led to the renaming of these wells and show us a great deal about Isaac's character as a man of God. As a special sign of God's favor, Isaac's servants discovered a whole new well that Isaac could claim.

Isaac's son, Jacob, dug the well from which Jesus would later offer living water to a Samaritan woman, keeping her from ever being thirsty again. Yes, wells figure prominently in these stories in the Bible. It should be no wonder that the well is such a powerful symbol of the life of the spirit. Because water is so elemental to life, everyone likely understands when we speak of spiritual thirst.

Physical thirst is tormenting enough. But spiritual thirst is even worse. That is when the world really looks like a cheerless, endless, hopeless desert. We need Jesus' living water more than ever before. Don't all people wish for a better and more satisfying life where the spirit is soothed by living waters? This applies to the religious and nonreligious alike.

Sometimes, when we are faced with a world that is like a spiritual desert, we realize that our spirits are literally dying of thirst. Worse, we find ourselves reaching for the wrong things to quench that thirst. This is easy to do when the flesh is so powerful and powerfully represented in the culture around us. We reach for the alcohol, the drugs, the inappropriate relationships, the solitary vices, and the secret, guilty pleasures that seem to quench our thirst but only leave us thirstier than before.

In the Christian walk of life, we experience mountains and valleys, lush fertile fields, and desert places. When we're in the desert places, we cry out as David did when he was in the desert of Judah:

> O God, you are my God;
> I earnestly search for you.
> My soul thirsts for you;
> my whole body longs for you
> in this parched and weary land
> where there is no water.
> (Psalm 63:1, NLT)

Less dramatic than physical thirst but far more long-term and insidious is when your heart becomes like a dry desert and you are thirsting for refreshment. Perhaps your work seems soulless. Perhaps you are doing something you never really wanted to do in order to make a buck. Could it be that your relationships with friends or family have become stagnant, pained, estranged, or broken? Or maybe you are at a crossroads in your life: facing your elder years, or just getting out of high school and wondering if college or a job is right for you. You may feel like you are wandering in a desert, with no signposts, no guidance, and no oasis.

This book is not only for Christians. It is for anyone dying of spiritual thirst who feels that life has lost its savor and purpose. It is for the individual seeking the Holy Spirit and the answers to some of life's most basic and crucial questions: Who am I? What am I? Where do I come from? Where is my life going?

Are you feeling like you've been left for dead in the dry valley of your Christian walk? Take heart. This book is your guide to thriving in valleys, digging your own wells, and drinking and giving cups of cold water. We want to walk in the Spirit of God through what Jesus and his Word have already revealed. Don't be afraid; God has not forgotten you. Ask and you shall receive the help you need from Him. Be encouraged. Be strengthened. Come and drink from the Water of Life. Be refreshed and experience the goodness of God all over again or for the first wonderful time.

We all get spiritually thirsty because we are spiritual beings. There is a life within us that must be satisfied beyond our physical needs for food, shelter, sex, entertainment, and material things.

Interestingly, while so many young people yearn for fame and wealth, thinking these are the keys to a good life, celebrities often find their lives broken by pained relationships, drug abuse, and unhappiness. Consider Madonna, one of the most successful performing artists of all time, who questioned her own spirituality when she realized that being beautiful, sought after, rich, and famous wasn't enough. She has it all, but even America's "Material Girl" realizes that there is more to life than all the things she has amassed.

If you're human, you have thirsts. As a child of God, you thirst for beauty, justice, truth, goodness, and kindness. You thirst for true love, for your life to have some kind of impact, for affirmation.

Simply speaking, you want to be fulfilled. All of these needs are spiritual thirsts. Everyone on earth has them.

Together, let's begin this journey to quench that thirst and learn how to drink continually from the well of living water. Only then will we never spiritually thirst again.

TAKEAWAYS

- Water is so essential to life that water and water sources are apt symbols for spiritual life.
- There are times when people experience deep spiritual thirst in a desert land of trouble.
- This book addresses those times and how to slake our thirst in a lasting way.
- People are spiritual beings, and they have spiritual thirsts.
- Among these thirsts are the desires for love, beauty, truth, goodness, peace, and harmony.
- Learn to drink from the well of living water so that you will never again be spiritually thirsty.

2
FACING THE DROUGHTS OF LIFE

God once impressed these words upon my heart: "Always be ready to let go of things before they get taken away." Have you ever felt an urge to give something to someone, but you didn't? Instead, you kept it for yourself. What do you hold back from the Lord and from others? Our tithe—the money we offer to God—is just one of those things. We also avoid giving our time, help, care, expertise, sympathy, and wisdom, often because we convince ourselves that we really don't have anything to give. Or perhaps we feel that no one would want to listen us or appreciate our gifts. When we do that, we create our own deserts.

Even if our hesitations stem from insecurity, it is never right to withhold from the Lord or His people. Those who hold back usually lose out in some way. Reluctance is often the root of our personal droughts. These crises tend to happen when we keep something the Lord wanted us to give. Because we didn't give it when we had the opportunity, it was taken away from us. This can refer to money, material items, and even relationships. We're not supposed to love anyone or anything more than we love God. When we do, more often than not, that relationship or that thing is compromised or destroyed.

So what do you do when things go wrong? When your finances crash, your marriage or family relationship fails, your reputation crumbles, or you lose your job? How do you survive such droughts?

Perhaps you are experiencing a drought right now: a drought of money, peace in your marriage, love in your family, domestic support, companionship, employment, or health. There are times when life seems empty, and you find yourself wondering how you got into the situation in the first place. You look around in your life, and all you see is a "parched and weary land where there is no water" (Psalm 63:1, NLT).

To demonstrate how to deal with life's deserts and thirsty valleys, let's explore the story of Isaac in Genesis 26. Isaac went through nine distinct "droughts" or crises. We will take a deeper look into the causes of those nine crises and how Isaac handled them. Just like us, he did not always know the reasons for what happened to him. We can learn from Isaac's many victories as well as his mistakes. But first, we will consider his background.

Isaac was the first offspring born in fulfillment of God's promise to the great biblical father Abraham. God had promised to give Abraham many descendants and make him the father of many nations. Prior to Isaac's birth, Abraham's wife Sarah was barren, unable to conceive a child. (Infertility is certainly a desert time, which is probably why an infertile woman is referred to as "barren.") Abraham had fathered a son (Ishmael) through one of his wife's servants, but he had no direct heir, and he wondered when and how the Lord would fulfill His promises to make Abraham's descendants as countless as the dust and the stars. When the Lord has promised that you will father many nations of people and influence the whole world through your descendants, facing the desert of infertility is puzzling! Abraham experienced a drought for more than twenty-five years until Isaac was born.

It Only Hurts When I Laugh

Isaac's name means "laughter" because Sarah laughed when the Lord told Abraham that they were going to be parents after all. Yet sure enough, in spite of Sarah's skepticism, the Lord allowed them to produce a child.

Isaac became acquainted with the real possibility of death at an early age, when God commanded Abraham to offer his beloved son as a sacrifice. Can you imagine how Abraham must have felt? Can you imagine the sorrow that accompanied the two of them as they made their way, father and son, to the appointed spot for the sacrifice? Did Isaac feel a sense of fear at his father's solemnity, sorrow, and curt replies? We don't know. All we know is that Abraham told his son Isaac that the Lord would provide the animal for the sacrifice, and then he proceeded to tie his son to the altar. There is no record that Isaac fought or even protested this strange treatment. In fact, Abraham actually raised the knife before an angel of God stayed his hand, explaining that this was a test to see if Abraham put the Lord first and foremost in his life.

That was a heavy test for both father and son. Abraham had to be willing to offer up his only child, and Isaac had to be trusting enough not to resist. (His actions foreshadow those of Christ, who also did not resist when His Father sacrificed Him for the sins of mankind.)

Once the angel of the Lord stayed Abraham's hand and God was reassured that Abraham would be true to Him, Abraham and Isaac found a ram with its horns caught in a thicket and offered that as the sacrifice instead (Genesis 22:13, NLT).

What kind of conversation took place between them as Abraham untied Isaac and they worked together to sacrifice the ram? What thoughts were in their heads? Once his hand was stayed, did Abraham break down weeping, embrace his son, and tell him the whole story? Did Isaac understand and forgive, or did he still have some fear of his father now that he knew Abraham was capable of threatening him with a knife? Apparently, Isaac was a willing participant in this incredible drama, making him a worthy heir and descendant of Abraham. If Isaac ever murmured about the event, it was not recorded in Scripture.

If Abraham had not passed this test, then he might have lost Isaac (and his heir and his descendants) in some other way. The Lord sometimes takes away whatever we love more than we love Him. In fact, the Lord said to Abraham, "Now I know that you truly fear God. You have not withheld from me even your son, your only son" (Genesis 22:12, NLT). We often lose what we cling to in place of clinging to the Lord. Yet because Abraham was ready to sacrifice what he loved the most to the Lord, the Lord knew his heart was right and restored Isaac to him.

This man was Isaac's role model. Abraham's shoes were big and scary to fill, but Isaac and his father's relationship doesn't seem to have suffered because of the incident. They both had faith, and Isaac became Abraham's descendant in every sense of the word, inheriting his father's blessings as well as some of his trials.

Our Trials

When we are going through trials, it is wise to first look to ourselves to see if we had a role in causing them. Were we withholding something? Were we unwise? Were we too tempted by what the world offers, thinking that, because we now had material wealth, an exciting spouse, cute and sweet children, or a second house on the beach, we needed God less? Did we love something or someone more than God? Did we stop praying first thing in the morning like we used to when we put Him first? Did we think it was okay to skip church because, after all, our child's soccer game was more important? Did we cut back on our tithes because the pastor said something we didn't like or because we didn't feel we could afford the ten percent? Were we "too busy" to volunteer our time, our services, and our love for others? How did we withhold from the Lord and humanity? Is it possible that this is the source of our losses and the onset of our drought? What mistakes have we made? What did we do to wind up facedown in sizzling hot desert sand, dying for a cup of cold water to tide us over?

A Psalm of King David says,

> As the deer longs for streams of water,
> so I long for you, O God.
> I thirst for God, the living God.
> When can I go and stand before Him?
> Day and night I have only tears for food,
> while my enemies continually taunt me, saying,
> "Where is this God of yours?"
> My heart is breaking
> as I remember how it used to be:
> I walked among the crowds of worshipers,
> leading a great procession to the house of God,
> singing for joy and giving thanks
> amid the sound of a great celebration!
> Why am I discouraged?
> Why is my heart so sad?
> I will put my hope in God!
> I will praise Him again—
> My Savior and my God!
> (Psalm 42:1-6, NLT)

Some of the droughts in King David's life—when he panted like a deer longing for water—were due to his own sins and mistakes. Are our droughts due to our own mistakes?

When Your Drought Is Your Fault

In his book *Failing Forward*, author John Maxwell says that there are no mistakes in life.

This statement is hard to believe when we consider our own mistakes or when we witness the mistakes of others. We all make mistakes. We are human. Yet in every mistake there is an "unmistakable" lesson, and that is how mistakes are turned into victories.

According to Maxwell, if you learn from your mistakes, then you pass the test of life and get promoted to the next level. If you do not learn from your mistakes, then sooner or later you will go through something similar again, or maybe your children and grandchildren will suffer in the form of generational curses. This is because you must learn something; you must pay attention to something. God sometimes uses difficult times (droughts) to get our attention so that we can learn certain lessons. If we don't understand the lesson and learn what we have to learn, we will be tested again, And next time, it will be harder.

Maxwell gives the five Rules for Being Human:

1. You will learn lessons.
2. There are no mistakes—only lessons.
3. A lesson is repeated until it is learned.
4. If you don't learn the easy lessons, they get harder. (Pain is one way the universe gets your attention.)
5. You'll know you learned a lesson when your actions change.[i]

If we can't pinpoint any mistakes that demand repentance, then we should seek to find out what the Lord is trying to teach us in a present time of thirst. Times of drought often have the deepest lessons to teach. For one thing, they humble us, and humility is a great lesson. There may be other lessons to learn from our suffering, though.

Sometimes we bring our problems on ourselves through disobedience. Sometimes they are all part of a larger plan. Sometimes they are a test of faithfulness or preparation for some greater task for which we will need the strength gained from overcoming struggle.

Even when we fall, God is there to help us get back up again. Like any good parent, He doesn't protect us from the consequences of our actions. He will, however, give us the strength to get through those consequences and to start over with another chance.

God is, after all, a "master of disaster"; that is, no one can bring good from trouble like God can, whether the disaster is of our own making or not. As Pastor Jack Hayford says in his book *Pursuing the Will of God*, "Even amid our muddling failures, the Lord can somehow bring about a net gain of profit, perception, and understanding. In the case of so many of the foolish, ill-advised, blindly or hastily pursued things I've done in my own life, not only did God bring me out of the pit of sorrow and despair, He brought me through with something in my hand that made me stronger and wiser than I was before I stumbled."[ii]

TODD L. SHULER

If you are in a drought and it doesn't seem that your own actions or lack of actions caused it, take a few moments to remember the Beatitudes. Maybe God is trying to bless you through your trials.

Blessed are the poor in spirit, for theirs is
the kingdom of Heaven.
Blessed are they that mourn, for they shall be comforted.
Blessed are the meek, for they shall inherit the earth.
Blessed are they which do hunger and thirst after
righteousness, for they shall be filled.
Blessed are the merciful, for they shall obtain mercy.
Blessed are the pure in heart, for they shall see God.
Blessed are the peacemakers, for they will be called the
children of God.
Blessed are they which are persecuted for righteousness' sake,
for theirs is the kingdom of Heaven.
Blessed are ye, when men shall revile you, and persecute you,
and shall say all manner of evil against you falsely, for my
sake.   .
Rejoice, and be exceeding glad: for great is your reward in
Heaven: for so persecuted they the prophets which were
before you.
(Matthew 5:3-12, KJV)

Are you suffering because of a system of injustice? Perhaps you are frustrated that one percent of people in the United States control at least ninety percent of its wealth while you struggle to make ends meet and worry about your children's future. "Blessed are the meek, for they shall inherit the earth."

Do people at work mock you because you study the Bible during your lunch hour and refuse to go out partying with them on weekends? Do you feel that you missed a promotion because you aren't "one of the guys" (or the gals) and don't enjoy talking about sex, drinking, pornography, or other fallen topics? "Blessed are those who hunger and thirst after righteousness, for they will be filled."

Do your children defy you when you tell them they cannot play a violent video game or go to see an R-rated movie? Do they say that you are an "uncool" parent and that all the other parents are nicer than you? "Blessed are the pure in heart, for they will see God."

Do others look at you uncomprehendingly when you make friends with someone from another background or culture because they believe everyone outside their particular group is somehow an "enemy" or not to be trusted? "Blessed are the peacemakers, for they will be called sons of God."

If you can see your own droughts in the light of the Beatitudes, then you can take heart and find comfort. To God, much of this whole world probably seems like a barren desert—at least as far as the people are concerned!

As it is, this world is not God's kingdom. We still live under an imperfect system full of injustices and shortages. This is not the world of peace, harmony, truth, and justice we all long for. But if you are facing circumstances beyond your control, if other people and "the system" seem to be ganging up on you, have peace. It's an imperfect world, and if you are trying to be a person of God, you will suffer for it at times (2 Timothy 3:12, NLT). You will be out of step with much of the world. That is to your credit.

What do we do when God withdraws from us because of these mistakes? Psalm 42 gives some clues. First, turn to God in prayer. Prayer is the starting point of discovering why you are facedown in the desert with no oasis in sight. It may feel like the last thing you want to do, and you may feel too angry and discouraged even to start, but know that prayer is the most effective way to get water in the desert. Next, have faith in God's Word. Once you've done that, hold your head up and praise God for what He's already done for you in previous situations and what He's doing right now. These important disciplines can help you get through a drought or a desert time.

TAKEAWAYS

- We all experience droughts or personal crises in our lives.
- Sometimes these droughts are due to our own mistakes.
- We can learn from our mistakes and change our future.
- God is a "master of disaster" who will help us get through the consequences of our own mistakes.
- Some droughts happen because of the way the world is right now.
- At such times, the Beatitudes are a wonderful source of spiritual sustenance.
- Whether our disasters are of our making or the world's, prayer is the way to find water in the desert.

3

TOUGH TIMES, SILENT SCREAMS

Although it may be the last thing on our minds and the hardest thing to do, the best strategy for getting through tough times is to pray, just as David cried out to God when his soul was thirsting. That's what Isaac did too.

Isaac's First Crisis: A Barren Wife

In Genesis 25:21, Isaac is confronted with the fact that his lovely wife, Rebekah, is "barren." Fertility issues can tear apart the most loving couples. Even the words "barren" and "infertility" conjure up images of a wasteland.

Couples with infertility issues often go through several pregnancies (and miscarriages); their hopes build up and then are dashed. They try embarrassing and invasive consultations and medical procedures. They experience grief and sorrow over their lost children as well as grief over the loss of their dream of parenting their own biological children.

It is possible that this short verse in the Bible implied all of that—the rising hopes that were dashed by miscarriages, Rebekah's conversations with older women about various herbs or methods she could try, the pressure on Isaac to produce a child, and so on. Rebekah might even have worried that Isaac would leave her for another woman because children, especially sons, were highly valued. She might have wondered why God chose her to be Isaac's wife if He wasn't going to let her bear children. Had their marriage been a mistake? Had the servant who chose her for Isaac been foolish to rely on the sign of a woman offering him water at the well? This couple must have experienced overwhelming pain and frustration.

What probably made it worse was that Isaac knew he was the heir of the promise of Abraham. A barren wife did not seem to fit that plan. At this point, many people would grow angry with God for making a promise and then seeming to revoke it. Some might decide that such an unjust God could not be worth serving. They might even stop believing in Him.

Not Isaac. Instead, he had a talk with God. He brought the problem before the Lord's throne. As the Bible tells us, "Isaac pleaded with the LORD on behalf of his wife, because she was unable to have children. The LORD answered Isaac's prayer, and Rebekah became pregnant with twins" (Genesis 25:21, NLT). Not only did Rebekah become pregnant; she conceived twins! Isaac and Rebekah had two sons, and God told Rebekah that these boys represented two whole nations (Genesis 25:23, NLT), all but assuring the couple that their lineage would be fruitful.

Let's look at four questions related to this crisis in Isaac and Rebekah's lives. (1) What was God's guidance? (2) What was God's promise? (3) What, if any, were Isaac's questions about the crisis? (4) What decision did Isaac make about the crisis, and what action did he take? We will explore the answers, add our own insights, and suggest some modern applications from the lives of these ancient people of faith.

In this case, I am sure God's guidance to Isaac was to pray. God had already promised a whole host of descendants, so some people might think Isaac didn't need to pray. But he did. Sometimes we need to pray over and over again before the answer comes. Sometimes we haven't yet learned what we need to learn from a particular desert situation, and we have to keep praying to find the right heart to receive God's answers (and sometimes that answer is "No"). Sometimes we have to take part in another spiritual discipline to get things moving in the direction we and God want. Fasting, for example, is a way to replace focus on food with focus on God (Matthew 6:16-18, NLT).

If God says "No" to our prayers, we have to realize that what we are asking for is not good for us. Some of our requests are not right according to the principles of God. Still, we can be sure of one thing: God wants the best for us. He sees deeply into our situations and knows the best outcome. He is anxious to connect with us. Prayer always helps. It never fails, even if the answer is "No." God's love is behind that "No," and if we search hard enough for the reason, we will find it.

God's promise in Isaac's fertility crisis was, of course, that Isaac would have many descendants after all. Isaac was basically saying to God, "Like my father Abraham before me, You said I'd have a lot of descendants, but so far Rebekah is barren. Could You heal her, please?" During his parent's fertility crisis to conceive him, Abraham did try to conceive an heir (and succeeded) with another woman – at his wife Sarah's request. Maybe Isaac toyed with the same idea of getting another wife, but his decision was to stay with his God-given wife and intercede with God "on behalf of his wife." This was a wise way to act on Isaac's part, and the results and reward were that Isaac and Rebekah had two sons all at once—twins! This double blessing was God's response to Isaac's faithfulness in prayer. In his prayers, Isaac reminded God of His promise and addressed the obstacles that stood in the way of its fulfillment. He didn't accuse God or say, "Hey, what's up, Father? You told me I was going to have a brood of kids, and my wife can't even have one." Instead, he prayed in faith for God to remove Rebekah's barrenness, and God did.

They say there are no atheists in foxholes. There should be no atheists in the desert either. Sometimes, when we hit bottom or fall down in the desert and get a mouthful of sand, we finally turn to God and ask for help, for guidance, for forgiveness, and for answers. When we find ourselves in a time of barrenness or drought, prayer works wonders, even if it we can only express it in the form of a silent scream.

The Lord hears even the silent yearnings of our hearts, but it is up to us to express and articulate those yearnings in prayer. Jesus encouraged the disciples to pray always and not faint (Luke 18:1, KJV).

When we pray in faith, the Heavenly Father's heart is moved with compassion because we are His children. Though billions of people live on this planet, the Lord knows each of us by name. As

Jesus told us, even the hairs on our heads have been numbered (Matthew 10:30, KJV). We are known, we are loved, and we are understood.

Psalm 34:15 (KJV) says, "The eyes of the LORD are upon the righteous, and his ears are open unto their cry." The Lord is watching over you with loving eyes and waiting anxiously for you to call out to Him in prayer so that He can have intimate fellowship with you. The Lord promised that if we seek Him, we will find Him (Matthew 7:7, NLT). Yet many times we seek the "Hand of God" and not the "Face of God." We pray "microwave-popcorn" prayers—expecting God to move mightily on our behalf with no effort on our part. Meanwhile, the Lord sitting on His throne is asking, "What about our relationship?" We can't necessarily expect instant gratification. What we can expect is a sense of peace and a burden lifted. What is more, we will almost certainly gain a new perspective if we pray with faith that God hears us and will take care of us. Evangeline Blood, a Wycliffe Bible translator, once said, "When we pray, it is far more important to pray with a sense of the greatness of God than with a sense of the greatness of the problem."

Have you ever basked in the presence of God? Have you ever sat there and felt His being surrounding you? At such times, it isn't unusual to break down and cry. We reach out in all the yearnings and silent screams of our hearts and express our longing to be with God and to be like Him. Our sorrow naturally wells up within us and pours out as we think of the ways we have rejected Him and hurt Him, as well as hurt others and our own best selves. At such moments, our problems dissipate, and we suddenly know what counts in this life—what takes priority over everything else: our relationship with Him. All things take a back seat to that relationship. All things—even our families—spring from and benefit from our relationship with Christ. That comes first; then everything else falls into place (Matthew 6:33).

Isaac's Second Crisis: A Desert Depression

Isaac dealt well with his first crisis: infertility. He prayed, and God answered his prayer abundantly. But Isaac soon faced another crisis. There was a famine, which is often caused by drought (Genesis 26:1, NLT). There was not enough food in the land, so Isaac headed toward Egypt for some relief, but the Lord told him to stay where he was. "The LORD appeared to Isaac and said, 'Do not go down to Egypt, but do as I tell you. Live here as a foreigner in this land, and I will be with you and bless you. I hereby confirm that I will give all these lands to you and your descendants'" (Genesis 26:2-3, NLT).

This is the second major crisis in Isaac's life. It is similar to one we've seen lately in our society: the massive economic downturn. There was a recession! There was no food, even if you did the work of farming the land. The flocks and herds were probably dying of thirst—no chicken, no beef! Perhaps like today, when plenty of able and capable people want to work but can't find a job, in Isaac's time, even the willingness to work by planting and herding didn't bring prosperity. It was a desert depression!

Isaac naturally thought of moving to where the fields were greener, but God commanded him to stay where He had told him to stay. God also made a promise that if Isaac stayed, "I will be with you and will bless you" (Genesis 26:3, NLT). He repeated the promise made to Isaac's father, Abraham, that He would give Isaac all the surrounding lands. God also renewed His promise to Abraham about making his descendants as numerous as the stars in the sky and blessing them with influence throughout the whole earth (Genesis 26:3-4, NLT). Those are big promises! All Isaac had to do was obey, as his father Abraham before him had obeyed.

Isaac might have asked himself if staying was the wisest decision. He might have thought it was smarter to find his own solution to the problem by going to Egypt, where there were fruitful fields and water. Still, he decided to obey God. We will see that the results of this obedience were good for Isaac. In God's math, communication with God plus obedience equals great victory, but communication with God minus obedience equals trouble.

A friend told me about a modern-day couple that had a nice house in the suburbs. They received strong intimations in prayer that they were supposed to move to another state where they had once lived. But they'd lived in the suburban house for more than a decade, and their accumulation of "stuff" was intimidating. The house needed work before it could sell for a good price in a tightening market. Both husband and wife had jobs outside the home; it was hard for them to imagine keeping the house neat and clean enough to have prospective buyers traipsing through or for "open houses" on the weekends. The couple disobeyed what they felt was God's directive to move.

They prayed and told God how difficult it would be to move at that time. They explained their concerns in detail. They could not imagine why He was asking them to move, and they laid out their reasons for staying.

Over the upcoming months, their daughter fell in with the wrong crowd. The family went through painful times as they dealt with serious teenage rebellion. Would moving have changed things? No one can be sure. Kids looking for kicks will find them, even in a new environment. But the move might have been enough to remove their daughter from the bad influences and help her establish herself in a new place, where she had to seek new friends and interests. Additionally, the husband lost his job in the area. Staying did not save them from unemployment.

Through the grace of God, the family came through it all and became better and stronger than before. But they suffered along the way. Could they have avoided some of the troubles altogether by obeying God in the first place? The husband and wife believe so. They are grateful that God helped them get through the difficulties their disobedience caused, but they still wonder if their lives might have been better over those years if they had obeyed God, even when it seemed inconvenient.

It is important to know that God doesn't ask us to obey Him just because He likes to see us hop when He hollers. He doesn't do it to make us jump through hoops. He does it because He loves us, and, unlike us, He can see what's going on in people's hearts. He knows things we don't know. He sees the past, present, and future along the same time continuum. He knows when factors are lining up such as a job loss or a child's rebellion. He sees that situation growing at work; He sees what is going on in the child's heart. He knows what desert sandstorms are gathering. We have to trust that when we get directions that don't seem to make sense and are inconvenient, God is thinking of our good. He may be trying to save us from the trouble that He sees coming, even if we are blind to it.

Here's an example of how communication with God plus obedience equals great victory. After several soldiers, including me, returned from the Persian Gulf War, a pastor invited us to his church to share our testimonies of God's goodness while we were in Saudi Arabia. We each shared how the Lord had preserved us through the many dangers we faced on the battlefield, had allowed us to share our faith with others, and had brought scores of soldiers to faith in Christ. We also shared how the experience had strengthened our faith in the Lord.

As I was wrapping up my testimony, I felt led to share the last command that my platoon sergeant had issued to me before we left our desert outpost via transport back to the port of Dhahran, where we were to catch the first of three flights on our return trip to the States. During our time there, we were grateful to receive many care packages from firms, churches, and nonprofits. One of these care packages was a footlocker full of Bibles written in Arabic and English. The military van was packed to capacity, and my sergeant could not bring himself to toss the Bibles into the fire that had been started to consume rubbish. He came to me and said, "Shuler, I don't have any room for these Bibles in the military van, and we're not going to burn them. Take a shovel, dig a hole, and bury them." I simply did as I was ordered. That's what you do in the Army—you follow commands, you do what you are told to do, you obey orders. It's good training for working with the Lord!

When I finished this story of burying Bibles in the desert sand, the pastor of the church suddenly stood up, along with his whole congregation, and they began to weep, rejoice, and worship the Lord together. My friends and I were mystified. We felt like we had missed some inside information. After all, it was just a story of obeying my last command in the Army, to bury a bunch of Bibles. What significance did it have? I didn't understand why I told the story or what it meant to the church; I had simply felt urged by the Holy Spirit to share it.

The pastor stood beside me at the podium, hugged me, and said, "God bless you!" As I took my seat, he turned and explained to us, "Throughout the war, we had special prayer services just to pray for all the troops deployed over there. One of our prayer requests has been, 'Lord, plant Your Word there.' Brother Todd, your simple act of obedience was an answer to prayer!"

The Lord's Word was definitely planted in Saudi Arabia. I literally planted it myself, with a shovel! I hope someone will find those Bibles and that they will come out of the desert and give living water to all who seek it.

My friends and I rose to our feet and joined everyone else in worship of the Lord who works everything according to the counsel of His good will. To Jesus be the glory, dominion, and power forever. AMEN!

I'm glad I obeyed that last order, and I am amazed that, through my simple obedience of a command, God used me to answer the prayers of a congregation and perhaps saved spiritual lives in the desert land.

In the case of Isaac, he made the wise decision to obey the Lord and stay. He passed up the "greener pastures" of Egypt and decided to have faith that, no matter how inconvenient and nonsensical it seemed to stay in a drought- and famine-stricken land, he would obey God, as his father had before him. Things turned out well for Isaac. He inherited wealth and prestige and blessings from his father, Abraham. Abraham was like a Rockefeller of the time, passing down plenty to his son. Fortunately, Isaac also inherited his father's tendency to pray and to obey the Lord.

TAKEAWAYS

- Prayer works wonders.
- Prayer must be accompanied by obedience in order to reap the greatest fruits.
- Answers to prayers may not always be convenient or appeal to common sense.
- God asks us to obey not to see if we will hop when He hollers but in order to give us the maximum blessing.
- In God's math, communication with God plus obedience equals great victory, but communication with God minus obedience equals trouble.

4
KEEP PRAYING AND OBEYING

Isaac found himself and his family in the worst sort of predicament—harsh economic conditions, crop failure, and a famine in the land. When he was a little child, his father Abraham had also grappled with the pangs of keeping his family alive. Having lived through that experience before, questions like "What should I do? Where should I go?" bombarded Isaac's mind. It might have gotten harder to obey God's dictum to stay in the land of famine when his kids were hungry or his wife was listless, with shadows under her eyes from worry, fear, and hunger. Sudden desperation might have felt like body blows from a heavyweight boxing champion.

"Every man has a plan until he's hit," said Muhammad Ali, and Isaac must have seen a lot of his plans crumbling around him, melting like ice in the desert. Faced with the possibility of total devastation, he decided to do what he had seen his father do in tough times: Isaac prayed and obeyed.

In Isaac's time of need, God didn't merely listen to him. The God of the Universe appeared to him, called out to him by name, and reassured him about all His promises. How that must have soothed Isaac's soul and given him "the peace of God, which passeth all understanding" (Philippians 4:7, KJV) about his seemingly nonsensical decision to stay in a land of famine.

In Dr. Kirbyjon Caldwell's book, *The Gospel of Good Success*, he encourages his readers with this comment: "When God calls you, don't keep Him waiting."[iii] Isaac didn't keep God waiting. He prayed and obeyed, and when he struggled, he received the comfort of God's reassurance.

The Lord says in Revelation 3:20 (KJV), "Behold, I stand at the door and knock. If any man hears My Voice and opens the door, I will come in to him and will sup with him and him with Me." To tell Isaac that all the promises to his father Abraham were renewed in him, God must have truly visited Isaac! I imagine God encountered him during a time when Isaac was praying.

I used to think that this passage from Revelation spoke only of the call to salvation—the one-time event when a person is born again. Meditating on this Scripture, though, I have come to realize that Christ wants to be invited into every part of our spiritual home: the bedroom, the den, and the deck; our hearts, our minds, and our "gut," where we tussle with soul-wrenching issues. Even those closest to us might not know the depths of our feelings, but the Lord knows. He's ready to come in, sit down, and talk about it.

Luellen, a friend of a friend, prays in her dining room each morning before she does anything else. She admits that sometimes she is sleepy and thinking more about her first cup of coffee than the Lord. Sometimes it seems that her prayers are not having the impact she wishes they would. But one day, something miraculous happened.

"I walked in the dining room, yawning," she explained, "and then I stood still. There was such a sense of Presence there. I realized the Lord was there, waiting. He knew I came at this time every morning. He'd gotten there first! It was then that I knew absolutely that He was there every day, sometimes earlier than I was, waiting for me to come and pray so we could be together. My prayers took on a new depth when I knew for certain I was sitting down at the dining room table with the Lord at the head."

One thing we can be sure of: even if we aren't always truly present when we pray, God is. He always shows up, sometimes ahead of time, waiting for us, His children, to talk to Him. He loves us, and He cares about us and about our concerns.

That's right. The royal King of kings, the Lord of lords, is willing to sit down with you and listen to what you have on your mind so He can guide you. We've been told, "So let us come boldly to the throne of our gracious God. There we will receive his mercy, and we will find grace to help us when we need it most" (Hebrews 4:16, NLT). We should never be afraid to approach God. The Lord is our "Abba," as St. Paul told us (Romans 8:15, NLT). "Abba" means "Father." It's a warm, affectionate term of closeness and family feeling. In the same passage, Paul assures us that we are the children of God, and we need not fear Him.

God knew of Isaac's anguish (just as He knows of yours) in the time of drought and famine. That's why He didn't sit impassively in Heaven and let Isaac handle his stress alone. The Lord came to Isaac to reassure him. Likewise, He is always present to reassure us in our time of distress (Matthew 28:20, NLT).

Thoughts on Prayer

Sometimes it's hard to pray freely. Emotions and distractions get in the way. You'll be talking to the One who made Heaven and earth, and all of a sudden you wonder if that ink stain washed out of the shirt you want to wear to work tomorrow. Your mind will wander to those delicious leftovers in the refrigerator, and suddenly you'll feel hungry.

If it's hard to pray, some people find it helpful to write a letter to God. It doesn't have to be long. If you have or have had a good relationship with your parents, imagine having an honest discussion with them about what's going on in your life. You can even pretend to call God on your cell phone and talk out loud in a private room. He'll answer! The Lord will honor any method you find to help you get over that lump in your throat and talk to Him.

Prayer devotionals, like *Our Daily Bread* and *One Month of the Well-Watered Life,* are helpful because they offer a format. Sometimes, when we pray freely, our thoughts tend to wander. A devotional can help us stick to the point and say what we need to say. The most important thing to remember is that God is home and God is listening. He's waiting. He wants to hear from you. He wants to help. He just needs you to ask.

Whatever issues you are facing, know that others have faced them before you, and some people have gathered thoughts, needs, hopes, and fears into prayers that you can read aloud to the Lord. This discipline may seem rote at first, but after a while, such words will take on depth and breadth and meaning to become a true cry from your heart. When devotionals are laced with quotes from the Bible or other spiritual sources, they enrich your soul with small, nourishing bites that may come to mind in a moment of need. Devotionals can help transform your relationship with the Lord and change you in the process.

What about unanswered prayer? Some prayers seem to go unheard, but I believe that every prayer is answered. Sometimes answers take time to manifest or answers are not packaged how we expected, but they always come. Another friend of a friend shared a story that her pastor told their congregation. The pastor was wild as a boy, and a neighbor lady told him when he was growing up, "You might as well just surrender now. I'm praying for you. You and that fallen lifestyle of yours haven't got a chance." And they didn't. He entered seminary just a few years later, called to be a pastor. If we are praying for someone else, they may be a little too closed up or closed off, but we can be sure that God makes the attempt to reach them if we ask Him to.

Sometimes God's answer is "Not yet," "That isn't what you really want or need," "That wouldn't actually benefit you if you got it," or "You need to grow in some ways first." But no sincere prayer is ever ignored. Whatever we pray that is within the will of God will be granted.

The Reverend Dale Bronner, pastor of the Word of Faith Family Worship Cathedral in Austell, Georgia, eloquently categorized God's answers to our prayers as "No, Go, or Slow."

When we hear "No," we sometimes become like children throwing tantrums. We get agitated. If you read the passage regarding Isaac carefully, however, you will notice that this is exactly what God told Isaac. He said, "If you're thinking of going to Egypt, Isaac, don't do it! Stay away!"

Until God ruled it out, Egypt seemed like the right place to go—it was a country with a booming economy, arts, and culture. Perhaps Isaac remembered how fondly his father had spoken about it. At any rate, he was familiar enough with Egypt to pack up the family without getting clearance from God to go. We need to answer the question, "Where is my Egypt?"

As tantalizing as it seemed, Egypt eventually became a place of bondage and oppression for Isaac's descendants—the children of Israel. Your Egypt is a familiar place that calls out to you when your world is falling apart. I know that I went to that place many times before the Lord saved me and brought me out of bondage, but "Egypt" still calls out to me. It's the place that seems like the easy way out of our troubles. It's often a place of carnality (lawless living that does not depend on God) where our feet willingly take us if we don't keep our lives hidden with Christ in God. I've got my "Egypt," and you've got yours. For some, it's the pity pot.

Debbie Macomber states in her book *Mrs. Miracle*,[iv] "It's okay to sit on your pity pot every now and again. Just be sure to flush when you are finished." For others, it's the psychic's 1-900 number, about which Evangelist Rita Womack once asked the question, "Why are you worried about your future when you cannot even handle your past?" For some people, it's the bar or the old girlfriend or boyfriend's place. For others', it's the marijuana joint. And for a few, it's a temper tantrum. Only you know where your "Egypt" is—the place you go for relief that has nothing to do with God.

Don't go there. It doesn't offer long-term help, and it often makes your droughts worse. It tends to cause future droughts too. Proverbs 14:12 (KJV) says, "There is a way which seemeth right unto a man, but the end thereof are the ways of death." When trouble comes, we want to follow our "natural" instincts, which can prove to be irrational and foolish. If you don't believe me, ask your spouse. My wife refers to my temporary mental afflictions as "dumb-nesia." "Dumb-nesia" is doing something dumb and stupid, only to forget why you did it in the first place. Before you rush to do something stupid, **STOP**, **LOOK**, and **LISTEN**! Life gets tough, but we may lose more if we turn away from Christ and go back into the world, back to Egypt.

The Lord is saying, "Stay away from that place. Come to My place instead, where I will be your refuge, your place of safety" (see Psalm 91:2, NLT). "I will show you where I want you to go," God told Isaac. It has been said that people give advice, but God gives guidance. I agree. God laid out the plan for Isaac, and the Lord has a plan for all of us. In the book of Jeremiah (29:11), God says, "I know the plan that I have for you," and it's a good plan of peace, prosperity, gladness, joy, and love. We simply have to bring our lives in line with the Lord's. It's His plan, not ours. When we completely surrender our whole lives to the Spirit of God, we become fine-spun threads that God uses to weave the fabric of His perfect will on the earth.

We find the Lord's plan for us through prayer. We get the strength to live it through prayer. We gain the wisdom we need to light our path through prayer. We receive the encouragement, insight, and love we need to do what we must do through prayer.

Don't neglect this important source of life-giving water when you're stumbling through the desert. Don't go to Egypt. Go to the Lord in prayer. The more time you make for prayer, the more room you will make for God in your heart and in your life. You can change your relationships, you can change the way your family gets along, you can change your economic situation, and you can change the way your boss treats you; it can all be changed through prayer.

But we must consider another truth about prayer. The movie *Shadowlands*, which portrays the marriage relationship of the great Christian writer C. S. Lewis (author of *The Chronicles of Narnia*, *The Screwtape Letters*, and *Mere Christianity*, among others), considers the role of prayer. In the movie, Lewis has prayed night and day for his wife to be delivered from the bone cancer that threatens her life. At some point, she achieves remission, and the two of them enjoy more significant time on earth together, sharing their love and devotion.

But then the disease returns, and Lewis knows he must face the inevitable—his wife's death from cancer. He remarks, "Prayer doesn't change Him. It changes me."

One of the greatest gifts of prayer is that, when we communicate with God, when we seek His guidance, His love, His care, and His truth, we are changed in the process. We take on more characteristics of the One to whom we relate. Our hearts become more peaceful, calm, accepting, pure, courageous, and loving toward others. We are better equipped to face the challenges of our lives. There is no challenge too great for God, and when we turn to Him in prayer, there is no challenge too great for us either, as long as we stay aligned with Him.

Prayer may or may not change your circumstances. You may or may not be delivered from the illness, the divorce, the debt, the difficult relationship, the pain of a loved one's addiction, the sorrow of a loved one's death. And if you are delivered, you may not be delivered on the timetable that you prefer.

Prayer will change you, though. If you are not delivered from the circumstances, you will receive the heart and the strength to bring good and a better future out of your situation. You will receive the strength and wisdom to deal with your problems and grow because of them.

Prayer is the beginning of taking responsibility for what's wrong, even if you are not at fault. Consider Jesus, who is the greatest example of taking responsibility for what was wrong, though none of it was his fault.

When it is our fault, we must admit it to the Lord in prayer as well. David said in Psalm 32:3-4 (NLT), "My strength evaporated like water in the summer heat," and the hand of the Lord "was heavy" upon him, yet when he confessed his sin and repented, the Lord delivered him.

If your strength is evaporating like water in the summer (or desert) heat, pray. God will answer. "Come close to God, and God will come close to you" (James 4:8, NLT). If you obey and pray like Isaac did, the Lord will bring forth water and flowers in the desert.

TAKEAWAYS

- When life gets hard and we face a drought, the last thing we should do is head to Egypt in disobedience to God.
- God doesn't just sit on His throne and see if we'll obey or not. He's available to guide, comfort, and reassure us in our times of drought.
- Prayer doesn't always change a situation, but it will change us enough that we can cope with the situation in a godly way.
- Relationships are gifts from God, and when both people are willing, prayer can make a bad relationship good and a good relationship great. The Lord is always present to reassure us in our time of distress (Matthew 28:20, NLT).
- Pray, obey, and prosper.

5

THE COMMAND, THE PLAN,
AND THE FOREIGN LAND

Long before spy movies and government cover-ups, I firmly believe
that the Lord was the originator of the "Need to Know" policy. He
tells each of us about the plan for our immediate future only on a
"need to know" basis. For the rest of it, we must have faith and
follow His commands. There are no crystal balls. There is only the
promise that if we obey, we will live under the canopy of the Lord's
protection and blessing. If we disobey, unfortunately, there are
consequences, even if they are simply a lack of fulfillment and a sense
of wandering for a time. This is unpleasant enough, but sometimes
the consequences are far greater.

We can trust that the Lord wants us to have life and have it
more abundantly (John 10:10, KJV). He is more than willing to show
us how to have that kind of life. At the same time, however,
sometimes we have to make sacrifices for His larger purposes.
Sometimes our specific benefit isn't exactly at the top of His priority
list. It is important for us to remember that God always works things
out for our good; but ultimately, for His glory. As in the cases of
Abraham and Isaac, sometimes God's plan involves an individual
person working on behalf of a people or a nation. Through them,
God prepared a people—the Hebrews—in order to send the
Messiah. The actions of Abraham and Isaac had significance for
more than themselves and their families; they also had significance

for the nation of Israel, to which the Messiah would come.

We all belong to a community, a society, a nation, a world. We have responsibilities in those spheres, even if we don't think about them much. Many Christians and devout people of other faiths believe that if America is immoral, then the nation will diminish economically and lose its power and influence in the world. Many people already see this happening, and they are right. The culture is more degraded every day, and respect for America overseas declines as more traditional cultures worry about American media influences and morals on their societies.

Yet America is made up of Americans—individuals like you and me. If we are not moral and upright in our daily lives, in the decisions and choices we make, we are part of that larger, degraded whole. We are either helping our country or hurting it in our own small way. There's a huge, horrific recreational drug problem, with devastating violence attached to every aspect. If each individual American chose not to use recreational drugs, the market would dry up, and the drug dealers would be out of business. The decisions we make as individuals combine to form big problems for our country and even for other countries.

It's God's world, and He cares about it. Don't we owe it to Him to obey His Word and His ways and do everything we can to live accordingly? We're not on this earth only for ourselves. We're here for God and for other people. When asked about the Law of Moses, a religious expert told Jesus what it said: "'Love the LORD your God with all your heart, all your soul, all your strength, and all your mind.'

And, 'love your neighbor as yourself'" (Luke 10:27, NLT). Jesus said that was right. "Do this and you will live!" he urged (verse 28). We have responsibilities to God and to ourselves, but we also have responsibilities to humanity as a whole, to our neighbors, to our fellow human beings.

In Isaac's case, he had already been told, as had his father Abraham before him, that his family and descendants would have an impact on the whole earth and on all of humanity. Isaac's family had a big mission, so Isaac's decisions affected lots of people, not just himself and his family. Thus his obedience or disobedience was even more significant.

We may not be an Abraham or an Isaac, but our decisions matter to ourselves, our family, our nation, and the world. It's easy to indulge in secret sins when we figure no one will find out or be affected by them. But that's a lie. Each of our actions has a ripple effect, like a pebble thrown into water.

For example, you had a bad day at work, so you stopped for a drink before going home. It turned into two drinks when you ran into an old friend, and finally a third. On the way home, you had a car accident. Everyone's insurance rates went up, and you may have hurt another human being and faced a "Drinking While Intoxicated" (DWI) charge that, in turn, affected your family.

Our decisions and actions have consequences. The decision to drink and drive has cost hundreds of thousands of people their lives. Some of them were innocent children who were standing on a sidewalk when a drunk driver jumped the curb. This is the reason law enforcement officers use Victim Impact Panels to talk to people convicted of drunk driving. The panels involve families and loved ones of car crash victims. They tell the drunk driver in person how the choice to drink and drive affected their lives, describing the suffering they endured due to the loss or injury of someone they loved. Our individual decisions affect others. In a very real sense, there are no private sins.

Actions have consequences beyond us. We have to ensure that our actions make a positive impact on the world. This means obeying God's directions to us, even when they don't seem to make logical sense.

C. S. Lewis wrote about the impact of our choices on God, ourselves, and others:

> Every time you make a choice, you are turning the central part of you, the part of you that chooses, into something a little different than it was before. And taking your life as a whole, with all your innumerable choices, all your life long you are slowly turning this central thing into a Heavenly creature or a hellish creature: either into a creature that is in harmony with God, and with other creatures, and with itself, or else into one that is in a state of war and hatred with God, and with its fellow creatures, and with itself. To be the one kind of creature is Heaven: that is, it is joy and peace and knowledge and power. To be the other means madness, horror, idiocy, rage, impotence, and eternal loneliness. Each of us at each moment is progressing to the one state or the other.[v]

The Lord told Isaac to pack his things and head to a foreign country—the land of Gerar and the home of the Philistines. Isaac had to make a choice. Would he obey or not?

I can imagine Isaac thinking something like this: "The land of the Philistines, of all places!" The Philistines were a ferocious people. Goliath, the giant that David fought, was one of them. They worshiped idol gods like Astarte (the goddess of fertility, love, and sex) and Baal (the god of the fertility of land, plants, and animals). They were not the kind of people you'd want for neighbors.

God told Isaac, "You will live there as a foreigner." As believers, we are all sojourners in a land not our own. We are in the world but not of it. In fact, to be a good believer, we have to remember that most of the structures of this world are not the ultimate structures in our lives. The Lord does not want us to forget this. In fact, 1 John 5:19 (NLT) says, "We know that we are children of God and that the world around us is under the control of the evil one." In other words, we are godly strangers in an ungodly land.

Sometimes we get frustrated with the worldly system. It seems that everyone is out to take as much of our hard-earned money as possible. It's frustrating that we can't cancel a cell phone contract without paying hundreds of dollars. There are fees attached to every kind of bill, from gas to electric to insurance, and they all add up. The bills are so complicated that we something don't understand what we're being charged for when we look at them. Life is often characterized by an ever-increasing demand for paperwork. As soon as we've recovered from the holidays, we have to do tax returns, and, if we have kids in college, the almighty Free Application for Federal Student Aid (FAFSA) forms loom every year too. There's a ton of red tape involved just to sell a car or to build an addition onto a home. These everyday annoyances are accompanied by shockingly bad news from the rest of the nation. We are all appalled by school shootings and other examples of more frequent and ferocious social violence.

Sometimes it is comforting to know that our worldly system is not God's system, and, while we live in this system, we are actually foreigners here. This isn't the way God wants things to be. To Him, this world is like a foreign land.

Iris, who is close to a friend of mine, told a vivid story about seeing firsthand how God is not the center of things on this earth. Iris's neighbor, Pattie, was a distracted single parent. She had a lot to handle, with four children, a full workday at her nine-to-five job, and a second workday starting when she arrived home to cook dinner, clean up, and badger her kids to do their homework. Some nights she probably had to attend a school open house or take the younger ones to the doctor. Single parents have to do it all, and it's rough. Nevertheless, the whole neighborhood was suffering from Pattie's three wild teenage boys. She wasn't able to set appropriate boundaries for these hormonally challenged young men! Each weekend, she allowed them to have long, loud parties at her house with plenty of underage drinking. Maybe Pattie didn't want them drinking and driving and figured she had to make compromises. But the beer bottles on other people's lawns and the sleepless weekend nights from the noise until 3:00 a.m. were almost unbearable to Iris, whose husband had to go to work early on Saturday mornings. Any attempts to ask Pattie to regain control was met with hostility and nasty pranks from her wild sons.

But Pattie had friends in the neighborhood who saw nothing wrong with her family's antics. In addition, when discussing the situation, other neighbors told Iris and her husband that nobody wanted to be the "bad guy." Although they were all disturbed, no one wanted to tell Pattie that she was letting her sons run amok. The phrase "boys will be boys" was an acceptable excuse for bad behavior. Worse, Iris often saw Pattie standing at the center of an admiring crowd. Most of these neighbors were men, and Pattie was very attractive. Iris felt chagrined. Why was this woman the center of attention? How had she drawn such a fan club? Her family's problems were having a bad impact on the neighborhood, and everyone was suffering for it. Yet she was admired.

Then Iris realized vividly that Satan is actually the center of this world and its system. She was not comparing Pattie to Satan, but the incident showed her that the wrong person is sometimes the center of attention and admiration. Our society trumpets immoral behavior as the norm. Satan surely doesn't deserve to be in the center, just like Pattie didn't deserve it. It is Jesus who rightly deserves to be at the center of our lives. Knowing Jesus begins with a decision of making Him the Lord of your life (Romans 10:9-10, NLT). That one decision can change your family tree. As a member of God's royal family, you will become a joint heir to the Kingdom of God through Christ Jesus

(Romans 8:12-17, NLT). Iris was comforted by realizing that this neighborhood drama was just a reflection of all social, economic, and political systems not being under the control of the Lord.

It can be comforting to realize that we are also in a foreign land like Isaac. This world's system isn't the way the Lord wants things to be. A wrongful power sits on the throne of this world. The hymn "Once to Every Man and Nation," which is based on James Russell Lowell's poem "The Present Crisis" (December 1845), contains this verse:

> Though the cause of evil prosper, yet the truth alone is strong;
> Though her portion be the scaffold, and upon the throne be wrong;
> Yet that scaffold sways the future, and behind the dim unknown,
> Standeth God within the shadow, keeping watch above His own.

Wrong may be on the throne of this present world, and truth may stand on the scaffold at times because this is not God's system here on earth. But rest assured, God has a plan to fix our broken system: Jesus Christ. Without Christ, no amount of social, economic, or political reform of human mechanisms will bring about a sustained transformation of hearts and minds. But if we are born again into the Kingdom of God through Christ's death and resurrection (John 3:7, NLT), we have become foreigners in this world and citizens of another world. We are citizens of Heaven. We now serve God as ambassadors to the earth.

Ambassadors are diplomatic officials appointed and endorsed as representatives of their nation by the government. For a time, they reside in another country as representatives of their home nation. As ambassadors of Heaven to this world, our duties include being light and salt (conscience) to the world and proclaiming the Lord's will on earth.

At no point in time are ambassadors authorized to set up a kingdom in a foreign land. To do so, the ambassadors would violate their orders and be subject to expulsion by the country to which they are assigned.

Throughout human history, new kingdoms could not be established until two kings waged war and a victor emerged. Before that war, all ambassadors were ordered back to their home governments until the hostilities ended. In like manner, one day soon, Christ the King of Heaven will order us home during the Rapture, and then the stage will be set for the last war of the ages. The book of Revelation clearly tells us that Christ will be victorious in this war, and His Kingdom will come.

In the end, the Heavenly side is going to win, but until that time comes, remember your diplomatic papers and your visa—salvation. We are to go about the daily business of being mirrors that reflect Christ's image.

We can influence the foreign land we live in, and we should. We can make a difference and change things for the better. We can stand up for truth and justice. Through faith, we can even transform our personal relationships and be a wonderful blessing to our communities. We should do all these things. Yet we are still essentially in a foreign land, under enemy occupation. When the structures of this world seem too oppressive, it is comforting to remember that our home is Heaven.

It's What's on the Inside that Counts

Many translations of Luke 17:21 say "the kingdom of Heaven is within you." King James, the New International Version, the New King James Version, the American Standard Version, the Good News Translation, and others all print the verse this way. My favorite translation is the New Living Translation, which says, "the kingdom of God is among you" (many translations also agree with this). Yet the King James translation is heartening. When we live in the foreign land, we have to know that it's what's inside that counts! We have to have our own kingdom inside us, because the one outside is not going to provide us with perfect peace, perfect opportunities, or perfect justice. Even though we must always fight for those things, sometimes a little Heavenly perspective helps.

Consider an illustration from my business life. I was working with a subordinate for the first time on a project. We were given a small conference room in which to work. I was the project manager, and I chose a random chair to sit. At the end of the workday, I left my notebooks and materials on the conference table in front of my chair.

When I returned to the conference room the following day, my subordinate had moved my things across the table and assumed my chair. This game of "musical chairs" repeated itself over the next several days. I found this frustrating, since it appeared to be an assertion of power. Why was my subordinate doing this? After all, I was in charge of the project. Why did she keep challenging my position and covertly my authority? Why did she feel the need to try to usurp my leadership?

As I struggled, in my heart God asked me, "Where is the seat of power?"

And I thought, "I don't know."

"The seat of power is wherever you sit," God said.

I smiled and relaxed as I realized that it didn't matter where I sat physically. The symbols of power in the world aren't important. The power is God's to give, not mine or my coworkers' or anyone else's—unless God grants it (John 19:11, NLT).

All authority is given by the Lord. If He has authorized me or you in power, we have it, and all we have to do is learn how to use it.

The seat of power is wherever we sit, even if we are sitting in a strange and foreign land that does not reflect the Lord. As such, we no longer struggle to get to power. We operate from His power. We who carry the Kingdom of Heaven within us have been charged with reflecting His Light into a world that is often engulfed in darkness.

We are in the seat of power because, as we discussed earlier, we have responsibility. We have the free will to decide or choose how to respond to any situation on earth. This is power. Will we be kind, patient, loving, helpful, honest, and forgiving? How we respond is our choice. That puts us squarely in the seat of power.

In *Man's Search for Meaning*, his book about being a prisoner in a Nazi concentration camp, Victor Frankl said that he still saw free will being exercised, even in an oppressive death camp. People chose how to respond to their situation. Those who became hopeless, bitter, angry, and conniving did not survive. Those who saw some sort of purpose to live for and to live toward, who believed that they would someday get out of their situation to fulfill that purpose, and who saw some kind of meaning in their suffering were the ones who survived. No matter what kind of situation we face, we always have a choice about our attitude.

Let's follow Isaac's example and accept that we are sojourning in a land that is not our own. Isaac went on to prosper and become an example of faith because he put himself under God's umbrella through obedience and because he believed in the covering and comfort of God. He went into the foreign land with the right attitude, and he prospered. We can prosper too, no matter what alien land we are living in or how little it may be to our tastes. If we are under the covering and comfort of God and are obedient and humble before Him, God will eventually bring good from our situation (Romans 8:28, NLT).

TAKEAWAYS

- God doesn't always tell us everything about what He has planned. We are to walk by faith and not by sight (2 Corinthians 5:7, NLT).
- Our actions and decisions affect more than just ourselves.
- It is best to obey God.
- We are all in a foreign and strange land, just like the place Isaac was commanded by God to inhabit.
- We are in the world but not of the world.
- Jesus called us to be light and salt (conscience) in the world (Matthew 5:13-16, NLT).
- The seat of power is wherever you sit, as long as Jesus is the head of your life.

6

THE COVERING AND THE COMFORT

"…But I will be with you and bless you," the Lord promised Isaac, even as He ordered him to go to a foreign land full of idol-worshipers and giants like Goliath (Genesis 26:3). Isaac was covered by the comfort of God's promise to be with him and take care of him, even as Isaac ventured into a less-than-desirable place.

Let's think about how Isaac might have reacted to this as a human being. I can imagine the lump in his throat as he sought to process what the Lord had told him. But before Isaac's thoughts began to spiral out of control, wondering what kind of rejection he would face in this new land and how the move would affect his family, God informed him of a security plan: God's covering and comfort. Psalm 91:1 (NLT) says, "Those who live in the shelter of the Most High will find rest in the shadow of the Almighty." In other words, the Lord's got us covered.

God would not only go with Isaac to that foreign land but would also give the land to him on behalf of his father Abraham's obedience. God said to Isaac,

Live here as a foreigner in this land, and I will be with you and bless you. I hereby confirm that I will give all these lands to you and your descendants, just as I solemnly promised Abraham, your father. I will cause your descendants to become as numerous as the stars of the sky, and I will give them all these lands. And through your descendants all the nations of the earth will be blessed. I will do this because Abraham listened to me and obeyed all my requirements, commands, decrees, and instructions. (Genesis 26:3-5, NLT)

The promise was not only for Abraham; it extended to his descendants. Sometimes we reap the benefit of someone else's work, obedience, and intercessory prayers. Someone may have paved the way for us with a covering of prayer. Someone may have stood in the gap (prayed) for us until we could stand on our own and seek the Lord. One of the more memorable campaign slogans from a presidential election was "A promise made is a promise kept." God never forgets His promises to His people. Even though Isaac's father had passed away many years earlier, the Lord's promise to Abraham existed in the past, present, and future. We may change, but God never changes. God is ready to keep His promises.

In fact, all of God's promises deserve the response, "Amen." As much as we say it in our services, we often forget the power and confidence this word expresses. Amen means "So be it" or "So it shall be." When it seems like what you're praying for has not come to pass, don't give up on God's Word. Say what God has already declared about your situation. Decree that the matter is done in Jesus' name, and punctuate it by saying, "Amen. So be it! So it shall be! Glory to God!" In other words, believe and affirm that it's a done deal.

As a student, I attended one of the local campus ministries at the University of Georgia. One doctoral student, a woman from Korea who truly loved the Lord, had been a member of that fellowship for many years. She fell in love with an unmarried youth pastor who was assigned by his local church to serve the university. Because of her cultural upbringing that a woman should be modest and shy, she was apprehensive of sharing her true feelings with this man. She took her problem to the Lord in prayer. Many days and nights, she prayed that this youth pastor would simply "get it" and understand that they were meant for one another.

He didn't. When it came to romance, he wasn't overly aware. Nevertheless, she kept praying and being there for this pastor when he needed to confide in someone. One day while she was praying, she sensed that the Lord would grant her heart's desire (to be this pastor's wife). She stopped fretting then and received the peace of God. Her praying style changed. Every time she felt anxious or fearful that what she prayed for would never happen, she chose to pray from her position as a daughter of the Lord by saying, "Amen." She asserted that the Lord knew what she wanted and that He would keep His promise to her.

One day, the pastor finally realized God's will for him in the love and marriage department: the Korean doctoral student! The young woman's prayer was answered and her faith rewarded. She is the pastor's wife and the mother of his child today. God blessed her openly for her faithfulness to private prayer (Matthew 6:6 and 18, NLT).

Try such a prayer of faith now: "I am (healed, delivered, set free, being brought out of this situation) in Jesus' name! Amen!" So it shall be! Proverbs 10:22, NLT says, "The blessing of the Lord makes a person rich, and He adds no sorrow with it." The Lord is setting you up for a blessing. He said in Malachi 3:10 (NLT), "I will open the windows of Heaven for you. I will pour out a blessing so great you won't have enough room to take it in!" How do you get the blessing? Many years ago, I heard a pastor on the radio say it like this: "When you meet the conditions of the promise, you'll get the fulfillment of the promise."

In the first chapter of Isaiah, God also says, "If you will only obey me, you will have plenty to eat. But if you turn away and refuse to listen, you will be devoured..." (Isaiah 1:19-20, NLT). It is better to follow God's commands than to suffer the consequences of disobedience. When we obey, we can heartily claim all the blessings He has promised us. If we do the right thing now, we can be certain that God will bless us and our families with His prosperity and abundance, including both physical and spiritual blessings (Galatians 6:9, NLT).

Isaac could live confidently in a foreign land because he knew that he was covered by the covenant of God and his father Abraham. In unsettling times, we need to know that there is a *sure* word for us from the Lord. Some people spend a lot of time asking whether it's God's will for them to do one thing or another, but I believe that God speaks to us through His Word, the church, and the circumstances around us. Sometimes He speaks through a person or persons. He may speak from an unexpected source too. Be on the lookout for messages from God, but always remember that God's messages will never contradict His written Word, the Bible.

One young mother in my circle of acquaintances told others the story of something that happened as she drove to pick up her son from a basketball scrimmage. Her husband was out of town on business, it was the dinner hour, and she faced four-lane traffic. Rush hour was still in full swing, and it was already dark outside. It was also the Christmas season, so shoppers made the usual traffic level even higher. Her mind was on the roast she had left cooking in the oven, her other children, and her husband, who was 30,000 feet up in the sky in an airplane. It all seemed too much. Then, to her horror, she noticed that the gas gauge was almost on empty! She had to fight her way to an exit with a gas station, hoping the stop would not make her late to pick up her son (or result in a burned beef roast). As she pulled in, an elderly and bent man slowly shuffled up to her. In a rich, Jamaican accent, he asked how much gas she wanted.

"Oh, fill 'er up. By the way, how are you?" she responded, in rattled politeness.

"Me? Why, I am too blessed to be stressed," the man said.

Suddenly, the woman burst out laughing. He was right! Why be stressed when there was so much blessing all around her? She had a car, money for gas, healthy children, food at home, and a hard-working husband. The traffic was already lessening as people made it home for dinner. Christmas was coming.

She took a deep breath, smiled, got her gas, and went on her way, feeling that the Lord had spoken to her through a little old man from another country whom she could barely understand—but who had carried God's important message to her just when she needed it.

Some of you feel stressed on Monday morning when you get back to work after a wonderful time in fellowship with the Lord and other Christ-followers on Sunday. It's hard to face life's tasks, demands, and stresses. Remember, though, that you are too blessed to be stressed. For the believer, your future is clear and your destination is sure.

With God, a promise made is a promise kept. Many of us wouldn't be here today if we had not had faithful fathers, mothers, grandparents, aunts, uncles, or other people who cared about us and prayed for us. Because of their righteousness and their relationships with God, we are here. God made a promise to Abraham, and He passed that promise on to Abraham's son, Isaac. Isaiah 33:15-16 (NLT) says,

> Those who are honest and fair,
> who refuse to profit by fraud,
> who stay far away from bribes,
> who refuse to listen to those who plot murder,
> who shut their eyes to all enticement to do wrong—
> these are the ones who will dwell on high.
> The rocks of the mountains will be their fortress.
> Food will be supplied to them,
> and they will have water in abundance.

God will comfort and cover the righteous person. We can be certain of that. The righteous will be protected, covered, comforted, and supplied. The righteous will have water in the desert; that is, "water will not fail him" in either a physical or a spiritual sense, for God keeps His promises to the righteous, even throughout generations.

Through our faithful relationship with God, we are to leave an inheritance to our children and grandchildren just as Abraham did (Proverbs 13:22, NLT). Money can be lost, stolen, or even devalued. But the inheritance of the knowledge of Jesus, when passed to the next generation, will never go bankrupt. The Bible says that the children of the righteous never go hungry (Psalm 37:25, NLT). In addition to the comfort of God's physical protection over us when we are walking uprightly before Him, we model for our children how to walk in a way that is pleasing to Him.

Isaac saw Abraham pray. He watched him obey God even when it wasn't easy. On the basis of that spiritual wealth, Isaac was able to become one of the great men of biblical history. He is part of an important threesome referred to again and again: Abraham, Isaac, and Jacob. These are the fathers of the Jewish, Muslim, and Christian faiths. We can see from this alone that the descendants of Abraham, Isaac, and Jacob did indeed influence the entire earth through these three "Great Religions" that sprang from the people of their blood lineage.

God explained to Isaac why He was pouring out His blessing upon him. It was because of the covenant God had made with Abraham, Isaac's father. The covenant was Isaac's comforting and covering. Both Isaac's God and the faithful obedience of his father (Abraham) had him covered.

Those of us reared in Christian homes probably had a mixed set of blessings growing up. People likely had high, perhaps unrealistic expectations for us. We might have struggled with a father who spent all his time testifying but still yelled at us at home when things didn't go right. We saw all his flaws up close!

In the same way, Isaac probably saw plenty of flaws in his father. Yet Isaac saw enough of Abraham's godliness to imitate him and to obey him. These and many other faithful people in the Bible set the patterns; they foreshadowed the greatness of Jesus Christ, the One to come.

We remember Abraham, Isaac, and Jacob because they put their faith in God's promises; they knew that He had them "covered." They were certain that God had their backs.

Do we have some of that faith? When God tells us to do something hard or to go someplace we'd rather not, let's remember that obedience to Him is required. God's plan is to be with us and to protect us in that foreign land, wherever it may be. While growing up, my dad (Reverend Allen J. Shuler, Sr.) would say, "Any time you are talking to someone that doesn't know Jesus, you are in a foreign land."

It may be a foreign land to you to live without drugs, alco cigarettes. It may be a foreign land to you to live without anger. It may be a foreign land to you to live without pornography. It may be a foreign land to you even to go to church. For some of us, these are lands where we haven't stood in a long time. It's terrifying to give up our crutches and learn to walk. But the Lord is with us. His promises hold fast. He will cover us and comfort us as we attempt to be new creatures in Christ and live more righteous lives.

TAKEAWAYS

- God keeps His promises from generation to generation.
- God will be with us and will cover and comfort us whenever we have to go to our "foreign land."
- God has promised to answer our prayers.
- The prayer of faith says "Amen!" or "So it shall be!"—knowing that God will take care of our request in whatever way He chooses.
- The inheritance of Jesus Christ will never go bankrupt.
- "Any time you talk to someone that doesn't know Jesus, you are in a foreign land" (Reverend Allen J. Shuler, Sr.). Share the gospel of Jesus Christ to people who don't know Him.
- God will bless you openly for your faithfulness to private prayer. (Matthew 6:6 and 18, NLT)

7

;GING YOUR FATHER'S WELLS

In the Bible, Isaac not only inherited his father's blessings from God but also spent time re-digging his father's wells. Enemies had plugged them up, but Isaac considered them important enough (and maybe strategic enough) to work to reclaim access to the water they provided.

We inherit both blessings and troubles from the lives and examples of our parents. You may have spent some time re-digging you parents' wells in your life, too.

If your father happened to be a preacher, you have your own difficulties to work through—your own plugged-up wells to re-dig. It's a cliché that the child of the preacher is the wildest kid in town. This may be because a preacher is a strong man and passes down a strong inheritance of do's and don'ts. In order to form his own identity, a son especially tends to rebel against his father. Yet, as with our Heavenly Father, no matter how much we rebel and deny our relationship, in the end the truth will come out. We have part of our parents' DNA. We are affected by what our parents said and did as well as by how they related to each other, to us, to our siblings, and to the world.

Speaking from the position of a pastor's family, I've noticed three types of preachers' kids (or PKs, as we are called). Some of them come through childhood unscathed and go on to have wonderful relationships with their parents as adults. Some are wild, "in-your-face" people who are against everything pure and holy, and they want the world to know it. Finally, some are inwardly rebellious and quietly angry, but they are outwardly cooperative, going along with everything Daddy says. Of course, the first type is ideal. Of the latter two types of PKs, however, the wild, in-your-face kid is easier to handle any day of the week (except Sunday). At least that kind of PK openly reveals his or her issues. The one who keeps everything hidden, though, will take longer and travel a harder road in order to bring these true feelings to the surface and be cleansed.

If we did not have perfect examples of the Christian walk in our parents (and none of us did), how do we recover? How do we take up our parents' torch and travel further in faith than they did? How do we reconcile the pain we may feel? How do we unplug the old, dirt-filled well so that it can flow with refreshing water on our own lands and in our own lives?

Many things your parents said and did were in line with God's Word, but you know that they also did and said many things that countered it. The Bible says that your own children will be your judges. Now that we, the children, are adults and leading our own lives, we can see more clearly where our parents succeeded and where they failed. Don't worry; your adult children will conduct the same detailed audit of your life one day. Yet, even if our parents were preachers, we must strive to see Christ beyond them and look to His perfect example rather than theirs. We need to forgive them for their failures and let go of the injuries of our youth. We do this by turning to Jesus.

Jesus is our Healer-in-Waiting. He will provide us with the water in the desert that we need: "Anyone who believes in me may come and drink! For the Scriptures declare, 'Rivers of living water will flow from his heart'" (John 7:38, NLT). Jesus also gave us a wonderful mechanism to help us let go of the past: forgiveness. He told us that in order to be forgiven, we have to forgive (Luke 6:37).

Whenever we feel like sitting in heavy judgment of someone, including our parents, it's time to remember our personal shortcomings. Were we the perfect son or daughter? Now that we may be parents ourselves, we understand how hard parenting is. It is difficult to make a living; pay the mortgage or rent, and numerous other bills; love a spouse; keep a car running; be a good citizen; take care of our domicile inside and out; and also be a loving, guiding, disciplining, and wise parent to children. Sometimes it seems impossible, even though as young people we might have thought raising a family seemed easy. Do we see ourselves in our own children's behavior? Now that we have a parent's perspective, we might realize that we were a bit difficult to handle at times. If you are a parent, have you ever yelled at your kids and realized later that you were merely reacting to something someone said to you at work? When the kids did the same thing yesterday, you smiled at them!

When we recognize the injustices we heap upon others, we are better prepared to forgive them for the injustices they have dealt us. If we forgive, we will be forgiven. If we do not forgive, we will not be forgiven. Forgiveness plays a big part in the parent/child relationship. Both sides of the relationship have the responsibility to let go, forgive, overlook, and weigh the positives as well as the negatives.

Sometimes, when a parent fails to learn the proper lesson, the next generation has to learn it and pay the price. This is demonstrated in Isaac's life. At one point, Abraham entered Egypt to escape a famine. As with many famines, we may suppose that this one was caused by drought.

Abraham told his wife, Sarah, that because she was so beautiful, men would kill him in order to have her if they knew she was his wife. At that time, respect for marriage was so great that a man would never take another's man's wife away from him. Instead, a man who desired another man's wife would try to eliminate her husband and thus make the wife a widow who was able to remarry. Fearing such a scheme and wishing to spare himself, Abraham asked Sarah to tell the men in Egypt that she was his sister.

Sure enough, the Egyptians thought Sarah was lovely, and they told Abimelech (the king) all about her. The king promptly asked that Sarah be brought to him (Genesis 20:2, NLT). Fortunately, it appears that before Sarah was violated in any way, Abimelech had a dream that revealed she was Abraham's wife. The king told Abraham to take her and go. He also showered Abraham with gifts out of gratitude that no one in his country had committed the sin of adultery with Sarah. The rest of the story goes like this:

Then Abimelech took some of his sheep and goats, cattle, and male and female servants, and he presented them to Abraham. He also returned his wife, Sarah, to him. Then Abimelech said, "Look over my land and choose any place where you would like to live." And he said to Sarah, "Look, I am giving your 'brother' 1,000 pieces of silver in the presence of all these witnesses." (Genesis 20:14-16)

Abraham seems to have gotten a lot of material gain from this incident in Egypt, but he was also quite cowardly. Abraham didn't want jealous men to kill him because of his wife's beauty, so he put her at risk. He exposed his wife to the chance of imperial rape!

Fortunately, the man in power, Abimelech, wasn't as dangerous as Abraham expected. He didn't kill Abraham in order to have his wife, and he listened when the Lord told him to avoid her. Abimelech was, in some ways, a righteous man. Still, even though both Sarah and Abraham came through the incident unscathed, most of us would say this wasn't Abraham's finest hour. We don't admire Abraham for hiding behind his wife's skirts to save his own skin. Abraham is exposed as a man with fears and doubts. In this story, the man of the "Promise," the father of many nations, decides not to trust that God will let him live long enough to see the promise fulfilled. At this point in Abraham's life, he hadn't grown enough in his walk with God to trust Him completely. He had to mature in God, as we all must do. We are able to read about Abraham's growing pains and can thus appreciate the man who eventually developed enough faith and trust in God to be willing to sacrifice the "Promise"—Isaac, his own son.

And Isaac went through a similar situation. As the Bible says, sometimes the sins of the father are visited on the son. Sometimes we simply pick up our parents' shortcomings and limitations through living with them. Character is often said to be more "caught" than "taught," and there are times when we must work to break free from a hindrance our parents faced so that we can be individuals. Psychology calls this finding our own identity; biblically speaking, we may simply be learning the lessons that our parents couldn't quite master in their lifetimes. We may be cleaning out and re-digging their old, plugged-up wells for our sustainability and success.

Like Abraham, Isaac had his beautiful wife, Rebekah, pose as his sister. Isaac's deceit made Rebekah vulnerable to sexual violation. The son repeated the father's cowardly act, knowingly or unknowingly, by endangering his wife in order to protect himself. (Later, Jacob, Isaac's son, did something similar when he made his wife Rachel and his children go ahead of him to meet his murderous brother Esau.)

It's hard to say that Isaac passed any kind of test by doing exactly as his father had done. It seems that Isaac had the same growing pains in the faith as his father had when faced with a similar situation.

Rebekah and Sarah were both women of faith, and there is no record of them being either unwilling to protect their husbands or furious at the men for making them vulnerable. There is no record that these events ruined their marriages. In both cases, God was able to rescue the couples from precarious situations. Maybe these women did the real work of restoration while the men were somewhat hapless instruments at the time. These faithful biblical women didn't take the proffered apple—a life of luxury in a palace at the price of being immoral. They stayed within God's will and were miraculously protected as they put their faith in the Lord and went along with their husbands' plans.

For us, the point is that some of our parents' battles will be ours as well. Some of the same things will happen in our lives that happened in our parents' lives. And we will pass some of our battles to our children too. As King Solomon said, "There is nothing new under the sun" (Ecclesiastes 1:9).

Even if challenges span several generations, however, we should strive to be known as great ancestors of faith in our families— examples to be looked up to and praised more than blamed. Our children will be our judges. We all need to try to live so that our children rise up and praise us. We should hope that they will want to be like us and will turn to us for wisdom, just as Isaac consistently turned to the example of Abraham. No matter what droughts we go through, we can try to view our parents with love, pride, and gratitude. When our own children strive to be like us, we will know that we, too, have lived a well-watered life.

TAKEAWAYS

- We are affected by our parents' lives and deeds. It is said that more is caught than taught.
- Most of us have a mixed inheritance when it comes to godliness.
- We must forgive in order to be forgiven.
- It is up to us to "re-dig" some of our parents' wells by purifying and clarifying issues or tendencies we may have inherited from them.
- Isaac imitated a bad choice that his father made, but God brought goodness and blessings out of the bad decisions both men made.
- Generational sins can and will continue until they are purged by God's help.
- Striving to be righteous and obedient to God will lead us to an abundance of living water.
- When you are out of the will of God, He will get your attention by any means necessary.
- Life experiences (desert places) will force you to mature in your trust and faith in God.

8
THE ADVENTURE BEGINS

Let's go deeper into the human emotions of what happened when Isaac headed off to Gerar. When God told him to go, Isaac put on his traveling shoes, packed up the family, and went to King Abimelech of the Philistines in the land of Gerar. He simply obeyed God and went.

As Christians, are we as obedient as Isaac was? A command is not an invitation. It's a command. Even your computer works by a set of commands. The late Dr. Cole used to say that invitations are optional, but commands are not. If the King of kings issues a direct, urgent order for you to go somewhere or do something, then it might be best to ask yourself, "What am I waiting for?" In any case, you can go on a journey—even on the journey of life—in panic mode or in peace mode. Your attitude is your choice. It all depends on how much you trust God to lead you.

Are We There Yet? Family Road Trips

When I was a kid growing up in Central Georgia, my family and I often took road trips to see relatives who lived in the Mountain West. My dad's military background was baked into his philosophy about taking vacations. Much to my mother's dismay, our trips were always low on everything: low frills and low cost. Dad would rather sleep at a rest stop than check the family into the nearest Holiday Inn. One particular trip to see my curmudgeonly uncle in Colorado is permanently etched in my mind.

It was a long and tedious trip. My siblings and I were playing a game of license plate tag. You win the game by finding the highest number of distinct license plates on cars from other states. Dad and Mom had packed the four of us (two teens and two preteens) in the backseat of a two-door Buick Regal. Midway through the trip, in Junction City, Kansas, the car's air conditioner stopped working. Did this affect my dad? I don't think so. Our skin stuck to the seats like Velcro. We arrived in Denver fourteen *long* hours later.

Still, I doubt if our travels were as rough as those of Isaac and his family. After all, we had a car, we could move fairly quickly, we had money, there were rest stops, and we had some protection under the rule of law. Isaac was in the desert, on foot or maybe riding a camel, with no rest stops other than a bush or two. Isaac and his family were subject to brigands and other dangers as they headed into a foreign land, where they most likely didn't know the customs and rules.

Even this great ancestor of faith probably had doubts. While traveling the hot, dusty roads on the way to Gerar, a dry lump must have risen in Isaac's throat, making it difficult for him to swallow as he pondered what awaited him and his family. Maybe he glanced at his wife and felt like the luckiest man alive. Rebekah is known as a stunningly beautiful woman who possessed incredible inner strength that must have made her even lovelier. When I read how commentaries describe her beauty, I can imagine that Isaac felt the same way Lieutenant Frank Drebin, a fictional character from the Police Academy trilogy, felt when he described a lovely woman: "She was the kind of woman who'd make you fall to your knees and thank God you're a man."

But Isaac's feelings of joy and fulfillment in his happy marriage were suddenly eclipsed by gripping fear and anguish. As we know from Abraham's story, it was not uncommon at the time for a total stranger to murder another man and take his wife. (Consider the later example of King David, who sent Bathsheba's husband to certain death in battle so that David could take Bathsheba as his own [2 Samuel 11]. David's method was subtler than others, but a man of power could get what he desired when he spotted a lovely married woman.)

I imagine Isaac was scared as he walked through the desert with his gorgeous wife. Maybe his faith wavered. Don't you and I waver in our faith, too? How many times have we desperately sought the Lord for an answer to prayer, felt God lift the burden, basked in His soothing presence, and gotten a sure word from Him, only to confront the same circumstances once we've left our prayer closets? We go right back into panic mode. Faith is easy in the closet, but out in the "real" world, it's a different story. Where we live is where we put our faith in God into action.

Next time that happens, my advice is to get back in the prayer closet and pray until you pray through it all, until you know beyond a shadow of doubt that everything will be all right. Open the Word of

God, find a verse that applies to your situation, write it down, and memorize it. Carry it with you. Put it in your purse or wallet, and take it out and reaffirm it every time you start feeling the quaking of doubt. Whatever you do, don't forfeit the peace of God. All believers need God's peace in this foreign land.

The song "What a Friend We Have in Jesus" reminds us,

Oh, what peace we often forfeit
Oh, what needless pain we bear,
All because we do not carry everything to God in prayer.

Remember these words. Just as Isaac's son Jacob later wrestles with God and refuses to let go without an answer (Genesis 32:24-31), you and I have to decide not to let go of God's Word until He intervenes in our circumstances and blesses us.

It's easy to say that "God is good" when things are going well, but when the problems seem to fall out of the sky like anvils onto our heads, can we still lift our hands and say, "Though He slays me, yet will I trust in Him" (Job 13:15, KJV)?

Isaac's Third Crisis: "My Wife for My Life"

It could be that the more Isaac panicked, the quicker he surrendered his victory in God. The moment this happened, Isaac's mind might have switched from self-sacrifice and obedience to self-preservation—a natural but unwise choice as a believer. This choice had the potential to destroy his marriage when he offered Rebekah as collateral on his bet for his own life.

"I feel a little white lie coming on," he must have said to himself. He was afraid that someone might kill him to get his beautiful wife, so he did what his father did with his mother years earlier: he told everyone that Rebekah was his sister, and he made his wife agree to back him up in his lie (Genesis 20).

Yet after Isaac had lived in Gerar for a while, King Abimelech (descendant of the first Abimelech, whom Abraham had tried to fool) looked out a window and saw Isaac hugging and kissing Rebekah. Abimelech called him in and said, "She must be your wife! Why did you say she is your sister?"

"Because I thought someone would kill me," Isaac answered.

"Don't you know what you've done?" Abimelech exclaimed. "If someone had slept with her, you would have made our whole nation guilty!" (The first Abimelech said nearly the same thing to Abraham about Sarah.) Then Abimelech warned his people that anyone who even touched Isaac or Rebekah would be put to death (Genesis 26:11, NLT).

In this third crisis, Isaac had a question. He wondered how he was supposed to survive in a foreign land with a beautiful wife whom other men would do anything to claim. He decided to resolve his question and deal with his fear by lying. God's guidance was to go to the land of Gerar, in spite of all the dangers. God had promised to protect and take care of Isaac. Isaac's response was to disbelieve that God could protect him well enough, and he tried to protect himself in a less than chivalrous way. Fortunately for Isaac, God intervened by letting Abimelech see the truth and respond with integrity.

Isaac was trying too hard. He should have "let go and let God," because he already knew that God had promised to be with him. Since Isaac chose to handle the matter himself, he sweated out a dangerous situation that could have ended in disaster if it weren't for the Lord's intervention and Abimelech's decency.

Trying too hard to save your own skin, your own family, your own relationships, or your own material possessions sometimes causes you to lose whatever you are trying to preserve. Again, we must be prepared to lose anything we love too much. By definition, we are not to put the love of anyone or anything before our love of God.

Why? It is because God said so. He's a jealous God. Jesus said, "'You must love the Lord your God with all your heart, all your soul, and all your mind.' This is the first and greatest commandment" (Matthew 22:37, NLT). In fact, nothing goes right when we don't put God first. That means the first thing we should do in the morning is pray. When the firstfruits of wealth, in the form of a paycheck, come to us, it is our duty to honor the Lord by giving ten percent to Him through the local church that we attend. We should also give part of our time every day to helping others in a godly way.

When things go wrong, then we must pray to seek God's solutions. His are always the best, anyway. Many times, we have a tendency to want God to bless our plans, forgetting that He is not obligated to bless anything that does not line up with His will.

When we choose to go our own way instead of His, God does not shield us from the consequences of our actions any more than a good parent shields a child from consequences. Somehow, kids have to learn, and as God's children, we have to learn too, no matter how old we are. Unfortunately, we often have to learn something the hard way. God is always ready to pick us up after we suffer the consequences of our ignorance and disobedience, but sometimes He has to let us feel the pain as a learning experience.

Consider again what happened with Isaac. He was rescued out of his situation. Fortune smiled on him because somebody somewhere must have been praying and seeking the Lord. A happy happenstance saved his wife and him. At just the right moment, Abimelech looked out the window, and, instead of being angry because Isaac lied to him about Rebekah, he ordered everyone to leave her alone lest they bring wrath upon their heads through sin. Sometimes unbelievers are more righteous than believers! Have you ever experienced that? In this case, Isaac lucked out because Abimelech didn't want the sin of taking another man's wife to come down on him or his nation.

"Whew!" Isaac must have said. "God really had my back that time!"

And God did. Maybe He remembered Abraham's faithfulness and Isaac's usual obedience. Maybe He recognized the merit of the father and the son in most matters. Perhaps that was why He rescued Isaac from a bad situation, or perhaps Rebekah's prayers and righteousness intervened on behalf of her husband after he put her in harm's way.

We don't know. All we know is that the promises of the Lord come true. God assures us,

> When you go through deep waters,
>
> I will be with you.
>
> When you go through rivers of difficulty,
>
> you will not drown.
>
> When you walk through the fire of oppression,
>
> you will not be burned up;
>
> the flames will not consume you.
>
> (Isaiah 43:2, NLT)

Even when we walk through a desert place, in a foreign land, the Lord will be with us and will look out for any quicksand we are foolish enough to go near.

TAKEAWAYS

- As we walk through a desert place, it is easy to lose faith and inner peace, but remember that joy will eventually come again (Psalm 30:5, KJV).
- We must be faithful in prayer. Don't forfeit the peace of God.
- God is not a cosmic superhero who removes us from all trouble. God's ways are mysterious, and sometimes we don't realize we've been rescued until we look back years later (John 16:33, KJV). Where you live is where you put your faith in God into action.

9
THE POWER OF ONE

Isaac's lie, while it may have seemed innocent, made his wife vulnerable to be taken sexually by another man. You're probably thinking, "What kind of a husband would do something like that?" In return for his lie, Isaac sought self-preservation and curried favor of the men who hoped to woo Rebekah, his wife. As we've noted, his father Abraham did the same thing to his wife, Sarah. Like father, like son! Remember that times were different then. It was not unusual for one man to kill another in order to marry his wife. Women were treated like desirable objects to be taken if one wanted. Maybe Isaac felt that he had no choice.

But the real problem with the whole scenario is that Isaac did not seek the Lord on what to do once he got in the city. He thought he would just "wing it." This is usually not the best idea. The emotional and physical strain of Isaac's deception might have placed unbearable stress on his marriage. Plus, Isaac likely had to bite his lip in agony and wipe the perspiration from his brow as he watched his wife, adorned in the finest garments and fragranced by the sweetest perfume, pass by him in the courtyards.

My wife and I were engaged prior to my deployment to the Middle East for Operation Desert Storm. I can remember the many days and nights that my heart ached as I yearned just to see her. Hearing conflicting dates on when our unit would actually return to the continental United States compounded my agony. When you miss your beloved, it can be devastating. During this time, Isaac not only couldn't be with his wife in the way he was accustomed to, but he had to live with the agony of knowing that at any minute, Abimelech might take what was his. Meanwhile, Rebekah's stomach probably turned in revulsion at the thought of the king calling her into his bedchamber.

The situation was turned around, and my theory is that Rebekah's righteousness played a role. She apparently didn't make a big deal about her husband's ridiculous actions concerning her (nowhere is it recorded that she tried to get on *Divorce Court* with Isaac). She handled a bad situation, brought on by her husband's preoccupation with self-preservation, with the dignity of a woman of faith.

It isn't recorded that she rebuked Isaac in any way. Maybe that was because it was no use talking to Isaac about some things. Maybe she had just read Stormie Omartian's mega-bestselling book, *The Power of a Praying Wife*! She seems to have taken the advice Omartian says the Lord gave to her when she had problems with her husband: "Shut up and pray."[vi] The same thing that had happened with Abraham also took place in the second generation with Isaac—the wife's virtue was saved, and the foolish husband went on to prosperity. It seems to me that this happened because the wife did her best to stay right with the Lord even when her husband didn't. Such faithfulness allowed the Lord to intervene.

This story shows some of the goodness that marriage brings into our lives. The Bible says in Ecclesiastes 4:9-11, "Two people are better off than one, for they can help each other succeed. If one person falls, the other can reach out and help. But someone who falls alone is in real trouble. Likewise, two people lying close together can keep each other warm. But how can one be warm alone?"

Fortunately for Isaac, when his own faith and prayer failed him, he had backup. Rebekah had his back.

If one person in a marriage is flagging, the other person can, at least for a time, be a pillar of strength in that family. For example, if one spouse loses a job but the other spouse is still employed, the family can probably survive for a while. If one spouse is seriously ill, the other can take charge of managing the household for a time.

Are there other times when one person in a family can make a big difference? Does your spouse or one of your children refuse to go to church on Sundays? You can still go. Don't make a big, self-righteous deal about it. Just go. Afterward, try to share your joy and inspiration with your family members in a natural, non-judgmental way. Go because it is the right thing to do (Hebrews 10:25, KJV). If you seek the Lord in this foreign land of the secular world, He will guide you. You can go to church. You can pray. You can fast. You can seek the Lord and His guidance whenever you get a chance. Soon, you may find your other family members uniting with you and turning to you for advice because you are peaceful, wise, and loving, and you reflect the character of God. You'll be a powerful influence for good without having to say a word—even if you are the only one in your family doing the right thing. Be that person of faith and pray your family through.

I'm convinced that, though they put their wives in harm's way, everything turned out all right for Abraham and Isaac because those wives overlooked the foolishness of their husbands. They chose to submit to the assurance that they would understand in God's time. They applied themselves in prayer to get through the period of testing. A praying spouse can sustain the family, even when the other is being foolish and out of the will of God.

Another story offers a biblical example of the proposition that you can change something—even a bad situation—by choosing to act righteously, even if your other family members are faltering. This gem of faith is about a couple named Abigail and Nabal.

Nabal, whose name translates to "fool," was a rich landowner and rancher known for his heavy-handed dealing and mistreatment of others. He was a man whom many loved to hate. True to form, Nabal's "trophy" wife, Abigail, the bronze-skinned bombshell, extremely intelligent and undoubtedly one of most exquisite women in all of Maon, saved the day by acting righteously in spite of her husband's foolish behavior.

Enter David, the young man who would be king, and his wearied band of men whose travels brought them down to the desert of Maon.

Consider the backdrop: young David was literally running for his life. His pursuer, Saul, then king of Israel, had been stripped of his kingdom by God because of his disobedience. Now Saul was relentlessly chasing David throughout the land, seeking to take his life at the first opportunity, because he knew that David would succeed him as king. David and his men sought refuge and hid among Israel's many neighbors and, in extreme cases, its enemies.

This time they came across shepherds tending their sheep, which were grazing in fields. The shepherds told David that they worked for Nabal, one of the wealthiest men in the region. Ever mindful of his mortal enemy, Saul, David instructed his men not to harm Nabal's shepherds and to protect them. Over time, Nabal's men grew to trust David.

Hoping for a warm reception, David requested that the shepherds take one of his men to meet Nabal, announce his honorable intentions, and ask for food and drink since it was a festival time. The shepherds obliged. Upon their arrival, the servant ran to his master and delivered a generous recommendation of David and his men.

What was Nabal's reaction? Warmth and kindness toward the man whose warriors had provided free protection against the bandits who threatened Nabal's servants and flocks in the field? Hardly so. Nabal held David and his men in utter contempt and lashed out at them in judgment.

"Who is this fellow David?" Nabal sneered to the young men. "Who does this son of Jesse think he is? There are lots of servants these days who run away from their masters. Should I take my bread and my water and my meat that I've slaughtered for my shearers and give it to a band of outlaws who come from who knows where?" (1 Samuel 25:10-11, NLT)

Stunned and dejected, David felt his disappointment turn into rage. And his rage turned into thoughts of murder and bloodshed.

"Get your swords!" David said as he strapped on his own weapons. Then 400 men started off with David, and 200 remained behind to guard their equipment (1 Samuel 25:13, NLT). David went to Nabal's house to take care of the nasty fool.

Meanwhile, Nabal snickered at how cleverly he had dismissed David's request for food. He had a party to plan. Little did he know that he was about to lose everything, including his life, to a man he hadn't even met.

One of Nabal's servants overheard David's plans. Instead of rushing back to Nabal, the servant frantically told Abigail everything that had happened and what was about to take place. (Maybe the servant knew that Nabal was too much of a fool to handle such important news.)

Abigail was worried. Four hundred hungry, desperate men bent on death and destruction were marching her way. After years of marriage, Abigail knew that Nabal was a fool. She might have realized it the day she married him. She'd already endured a lot because of him. She probably wanted to mount her horse, take her treasures and handmaidens, and head for the hills. But she didn't do that. She behaved virtuously.

She knew who David was. She knew that David would become king of all Israel. Without thinking twice, Abigail dropped everything she was doing and moved with a sense of urgency. She opened Nabal's finest storehouses and sent a meal that was "fit for a king" to David and his men. Check out this spread:

200 loaves of bread

2 wineskins of the finest wine

5 plump "fully seasoned, heat and serve" sheep

A bushel of the finest roasted grains

100 raisin cakes

200 "Fig Newtons"

Abigail sent all of this to David on the back of a donkey as a welcoming gift. She also spruced up a little, probably sprayed a bit of eau de toilette, and raced out to meet the future king in person. In fact, when she saw David, she got off her donkey and bowed all the way down with her face to the ground (1 Samuel 25:23, NLT). David was both moved and grateful that, by her graciousness, Abigail had kept him from shedding blood that day.

Abigail knew her husband. She realized their predicament, and she took matters into her own hands. She gave her best. She went out to meet David, her husband's mortal enemy, at the crossroads, got on her hands and knees, and pleaded for her husband's life. "I accept all blame in this matter, my lord," she said to David. "Please listen to what I have to say. I know Nabal is a wicked and ill-tempered man; please don't pay any attention to him. He is a fool, just as his name suggests. But I never even saw the young men you sent" (1 Samuel

25:24-25, NLT). Abigail also reminded him that the battle was not his but God's, and God had a throne awaiting him as a king. That simple reminder of truth caused David's knees to buckle. The anger that chiseled his face melted into tears of relief and repentance. How could he forget the Lord who had brought him this far and had spared his life? Why did he need more blood on his hands just because a fool had insulted him? Abigail soothed his soul and his anger.

Then she returned home, thankful to God and to David for their mercy. As a virtuous wife, she accompanied her husband to his dinner party. She waited to break the news to him another day because, that evening, Nabal and friends feasted and partied the night away.

The next morning, when her husband sobered up, I like to imagine that Abigail and Nabal had a conversation like this:

Abigail: Honey, I need to speak with you for a moment.

Nabal: Oh, Abigail, can't you see I'm dealing with a severe hangover? What do you want now?

Abigail: Well, sweetheart, I just needed to tell you that yesterday, I had to take some steps to save our family.

Nabal: What? What do you mean?

Abigail: Do you remember the men who came to ask for food?

Nabal: Yes, I remember those losers—the ones who said they came in the name of some idiot by the name of David. They said he had generously protected my men and sheep and wanted something in return. I gave them a piece of my mind and told them to get out of my face. So what?

Abigail: Those men went back and told David—who is going to be king someday, you may recall—what you said. It upset him so much that he brought 400 of his men to wipe us out.

Nabal: You've got to be kidding!

Abigail: No. I'm not. They were in striking distance when I ran out to meet them.

Nabal: Why didn't you come and get me?

Abigail: Because I heard what you did earlier, and I did not want you to come into harm's way.

Nabal: So what did you do, Abigail? Tell me that.

Abigail: I gave them what they wanted. Food. As much as I could load on a donkey. (*Abigail enumerates the list of things she sent.*)

Nabal *(fuming)*: You did what? How could you? That was some of my finest food. How could you give my best to a total stranger? Don't you know how much I've sacrificed?

Abigail *(pleading)*: But Nabal, he was going to kill you, and had he done so, we wouldn't be having this conversation. Besides, we had more than enough to share.

Nabal: That's not the point! It belonged to me! It was all mine! How could y-y-you...ugh!"

With that, Nabal slumped over and crashed to the floor, felled by a massive heart attack. Ten days later, he died. David heard about Nabal's quick death and repented yet again to the Lord. David was glad that the Lord had avenged him on Nabal so that he avoided shedding any blood. It was enough to slay the tens of thousands that Saul was so jealous about; he didn't need civilian blood on his hands, too.

Then David started thinking about Abigail. "How can I forget a woman like Abigail?" he may have wondered. "She's gorgeous, intelligent, and godly. She's suffered under that nitwit, Nabal, and yet remained patient and kind. A woman like her deserves to be my queen."

So instead of sending his condolences or a wreath, David sent a message to Abigail, asking her to be his wife.

Of course, nobody can promise that if you do the right thing, even when your spouse or someone you love is acting like a fool, you will be lifted out of the desert by a handsome prince who writes killer poetry. For wives, it may be that by doing the right thing and staying in prayer, your "Nabal" becomes a "King David" in your own household, as your prayers soften and change him and fill him with the wisdom of God. For husbands, your wife may not become like Abigail—gorgeous, smart, sacrificial, and ready to save you even when you've acted like an idiot. But rest assured that things will get better the more both of you seek to align yourselves with God through prayer and become easier to love and easier to live with.

It worked for Abraham. It worked for Isaac. It worked for them even when they made some missteps and acted like cowards in relation to their wives. It worked for Abigail, who saved her husband's life with her actions. It worked for David, whose hand was stayed from shedding more blood. David had the satisfaction of being avenged by the Lord Himself. And later he became king of Israel and wrote about his relationship with God so poignantly that we still refer to his words today for guidance in approaching the Lord of Hosts (the book of Psalms).

Praying and aligning yourself with God's will and God's ways will bring you blessings, even if you are the only one who is faithful. You'll be protected, as will the ones you love, even when they mess up like Abraham, Isaac, and David did at times. You and your family will be protected even if you are the only one going down on your knees to pray. God sees you and hears you. That's the power of one person living righteously for God. Such a person is truly an oasis in the desert.

TAKEAWAYS

- A family may go through repeated "tests" and "trials," yet even one righteous and praying member can pull the family through.
- "The effectual fervent prayers of a righteous man availeth much" (James 5:16, KJV).
- A spouse is a blessing; we all need someone to help us get up when we are down. God will reward you openly for your faithfulness to private prayer.
- You can become an oasis in the desert by being a person of prayer in your family.

10
PLANTING AND HARVESTING
AN ABUNDANT CROP

You may have heard of immigrants who came to the United States with nothing and became millionaires. Did you ever wonder how foreigners could come to this country with so little and still be successful? Immigrants who began as laborers or working for minimum wage in convenience stores have somehow put their kids through college and started a professional generation—all in twenty or thirty years, in a culture they didn't understand, working with a language they did not speak. How did they become successful when many Americans born and raised here have not been able to do so? America is truly the land of opportunity—the land of potential.

There are many answers, of course. But one reason might be that some immigrants use their God-given talents and are virtuous in ways that please the Lord, so the Lord blesses them mightily. Maybe immigrants work harder because they know they are at a disadvantage. Maybe they sacrifice more. Maybe God has compassion on them because they can't speak the language, their clothes are strange and unfashionable, and their overcrowded houses smell of spices and cooking from the old country, and everyone in their neighborhood makes fun of them and calls them names.

Yet these kinds of people often make it: they work night and day, send their kids to college, move out of the city into the suburbs with big green lawns, and do everything they can to work their way up. They often bring virtues that may seem old-fashioned in modern-day America, but they are actually godly qualities like virginity before marriage, fidelity afterward, respect for elders and the extended family, hard work, thrift, saving for a rainy day, honesty, decency, and tight-knit family and community bonds. The Lord blesses many immigrants accordingly. My wife's stepfather is the child of an immigrant. His father came to America in 1915 with nothing more than the clothes on his back. I assumed he immigrated for the same reasons as Abraham and Isaac: self-preservation and the opportunity of prosperity.

Isaac, a stranger in a strange land, a foreigner, and an immigrant, planted grain and had a good harvest the first year. The Lord blessed him, and Isaac was so successful that he became rich. Because Isaac obeyed God and went to the land of the Philistines, God allowed him to prosper in the midst of his enemies. Isn't that like God? He tends to pull us through when we've stepped into the lion's den in faith. I don't imagine it is easy for immigrants to first hear in their hearts, "Go to America, the land of the free and the home of the brave." Yet they pick up and go to the country whose motto is "In God We Trust" and that was founded by people who came to its shores seeking freedom to worship the Lord in the way they were called.

David said of the Lord in Psalm 23:5 (NLT), "You prepare a feast for me in the presence of my enemies. You honor me by anointing my head with oil. My cup overflows with blessings." That's abundance.

Abundance comes from the Lord, and this applies to far more than money. Abundance means knowing that all your needs will be answered and then some. It means being appreciative and joyful about what you have and knowing that the glass is half full rather than half empty. It means knowing that you live under the umbrella of God's protection, understanding, and support. It means living in love with your family members. In *The Shelter of Each Other*, psychologist Mary Pipher says that she measures a family's wealth by how many sunsets they've watched together in the past year.[vii] *That* is abundance.

Abundance means having a well-watered life in every way. It is described in Jeremiah 17:7-8 (NLT):

> But blessed are those who trust in the LORD
>
> and have made the LORD their hope and confidence.
>
> They are like trees planted along a riverbank,
>
> with roots that reach deep into the water.
>
> Such trees are not bothered by the heat
>
> or worried by long months of drought.
>
> Their leaves stay green,
>
> and they never stop producing fruit.

The kind of abundance that comes from hard work, sacrifice, and virtue can't be taken away. Along with accumulating riches (in their various forms) on earth, our true wealth is accumulated in Heaven: "Store your treasures in Heaven, where moths and rust cannot destroy, and thieves do not break in and steal" (Matthew 6:20, NLT).

Many of us long for what we don't have and envy what "Brother Jones" has. But are we using our God-given talents and skills as effectively as Brother Jones is? Are we using our gifts as effectively as those foreigners—those strangers in a strange land—who are working night and day in a culture not their own and succeeding at it too?

When Moses and the children of Israel were trapped between the Red Sea and the Egyptians, Moses cried out to the Lord to help him. God answered Moses, "Why are you crying out to me? Tell the people to get moving! Pick up your staff and raise your hand over the sea. Divide the water so the Israelites can walk through the middle of the sea on dry ground" (Exodus 14:16, NLT).

We have to use what God and our parents gave us. Some people are good with their hands, while others are creative thinkers and designers. Some people are good with numbers, while others work better with words. Look for your inborn talents, and do everything you can to develop them so that they are useful and marketable. If it means taking courses to learn more, then take them. Grants and loans are available if you need assistance. Do everything to improve yourself. Pray, and have faith that your hard work will pay off.

Some of us are clinging to dead-end jobs that are not challenging and don't necessarily pay well. We need to ask God for wisdom and courage to move forward.

Here is God's Definition of Prosperity:

Prosperity (Success) = Obedience + Knowledge + Faith + Work + God's Blessing

Isaac became a wealthy man when the Lord blessed him, as He blessed his father before him, because both he and his father tried hard to be righteous men. Although they made mistakes, Abraham and Isaac were faithful and obedient to the Lord, and He prospered their endeavors.

Isaac's Fourth Crisis: Trying to Prosper in a Strange Land

When Isaac first went to Gerar, he faced an economic crisis— namely, how to make a living in this new land. No doubt he brought a "starter" herd and flock with him, but he didn't know how hospitable the people or the terrain would be. He might have wondered if he should go to Gerar Community College and learn a new trade that would be more valued and marketable in his new surroundings.

Instead, he decided to use what he had in the best way he could. Just like foreigners who come to America and use what they have to the best of their abilities, Isaac prospered. He knew that God had promised to bless him and give him plenty of descendants and land. Surely God knew that Isaac would need cash crops to afford to maintain his blessings. Isaac's response was to do what his father had taught him to do—he raised herds and flocks, and they multiplied with God's blessing upon him. He prospered and became wealthy and influential. You can imagine that he created quite a few jobs in Gerar for unemployed sheep and goat herders. In fact, Isaac became so wealthy that the Philistines were jealous, so they stopped up the wells that Abraham's servants had dug before his death.

Wells were so crucial to life in the desert that stopping up someone's well was an act of war. Isaac needed well water for his herds, flocks, and crops. He needed it for his family's survival. He needed the wells to establish ownership of the land. The wells were his property markers.

Isaac had solved the crisis of how to make a living in Gerar. He used what he had and what he knew, applied his skills along with his diligence, and became successful in a foreign land. However, Isaac had no control over how his prosperity, as an immigrant, incited feelings of envy in others.

Now, Isaac faced a new crisis. Abimelech told Isaac that he had become too powerful to hang around any longer and demanded that he leave Gerar. Isaac had to decide what to do now that his hard-won peace and prosperity were threatened.

This can happen in our lives too. Has the enemy thrown dirt down your well and declared war on you and your family? Is your access to the living water—to Jesus—blocked? Do you find yourself in a desert place? If so, don't give up hope. It is time for you to decide to defend your wells and/or dig new ones to reclaim the land.

TAKEAWAYS

- Abundance comes from the Lord, and it appears in many forms.
- Remember to use what God has already placed in your hands.
- God's Definition of Prosperity is Success = Obedience + Knowledge + Faith + Work + God's Blessing.
- It is time for you to decide to defend your wells and/or dig new ones to reclaim the land.

11
"GET OUT OF DODGE"

Isaac's Fifth Crisis: Choosing to Fold *and* Hold

Isaac's wells were being sabotaged. The jealously and strife over his success was reaching a climax. This desperate situation threw Isaac into a fifth crisis. For the sake of peace, Abimelech told Isaac to leave Gerar. After working so hard, he must have felt like a leaky balloon: deflated and disappointed. His emotions must have been raw. He probably felt a lot of anger and frustration. This land was supposed to belong to him, according to God's promise. He'd already come such a long way and been through so much. It wasn't easy to prosper as a herder out in the desert. Now it would all be taken from him because a bunch of Philistines were jealous of his success.

What do you do when you are living the promise of God and then suddenly you're not? What should Isaac do? Should he stay and fight? Should he move away—slink out of Gerar with his tail between his legs, as if he had done something shameful? Should he use his power, wealth, and influence to dethrone Abimelech and set himself up as king? Should he stop up some of the Philistines' wells in an eye-for-an-eye and a tooth-for-a-tooth retaliation scheme? Or should he begin again, staying out of the city but painstakingly cleaning out his father's wells?

In Kenny Rogers's song "The Gambler," the Gambler tells the younger man that he has to "know when to hold 'em, know when to fold 'em, know when to walk away and know when to run." Isaac had to know this as well. He decided to fold up his operation and move out to the Valley of Gerar, where he settled near his father's old lands, re-dug Abraham's wells, and gave them the same names. Isaac chose to start over. He walked away—but he didn't run. Isaac decided to fold some of his cards by moving further out in the valley, but he held other cards in the form of his father's old wells. He chose not to wallow in self-pity over the unfair situation. Instead, Isaac began again, digging out those old wells, reclaiming and honoring his father's work and the Lord's promises to him. Isaac also told his servants to keep looking for water.

We can live by his example. Instead of worrying about things we've lost, we can keep pressing our way to Jesus. With Him, we will find new blessings and a fresh anointing. We will discover and establish new wells.

The Lord blessed the efforts of Isaac's servants, and they found a new well. This was a good sign! Isaac was going to lead a well-watered life after all, because despite his difficulties, he had a new source of water. Unfortunately, the envy of others brought another crisis his way.

Isaac's Sixth Crisis: Choosing His Battles

Isaac relocated and rediscovered his father's wells. His hardy servants also found a new well of fresh water, which probably signifies that God supported Isaac's move to keep the peace. But the herdsman of the Valley of Gerar quarreled with Isaac's herdsman, so Isaac named the well "Argument" (Genesis 26:18-20, NLT). Then, when his men dug another well, the Philistines were mad about that one too, so Isaac named it "Enmity" (Genesis 26:21 NIV) and moved on. Finally, he found a space where the others left him alone, with plenty of land. No one bothered him about the well he dug there, so he named it "Plenty of Room" and prophesied that now they would "flourish in the land" (Genesis 26:22, NIV).

Isaac chose his battles (or rather, chose not to battle) and tried to accommodate the people who kept bothering him. Whenever they gave him trouble, he simply moved on. Crisis resolved. Or was it crisis deferred?

Isaac's Seventh Crisis: Uneasy in the Open

Isaac must have been uneasy. He and his family were in the wide-open spaces, quarreling about water rights for their herds and land. Where I live, Georgia and Tennessee have been engaged in a long-standing battle over property and water rights stemming from an 1818 land survey. Unfortunately for Isaac, there wasn't much of a sheriff around, unless you count Abimelech. Having moved his whole household, Isaac must have been somewhat vulnerable, too. His wife was with him. His children were with him. They had servants, no doubt some of them women or perhaps older men or people who were not entirely able-bodied. No doubt Isaac had a strong force of people with him, too, but he was, after all, out in the middle of nowhere.

Still, Isaac's heart must have remained faithful, because the good Lord appeared to him that night and reassured him. The Lord affirmed that He was with Isaac, that He was the God of his father Abraham, and that Isaac would enjoy many descendants and inherit the promises made to his father. God's reassurance helped resolve Isaac's crisis of uneasiness. It was an affirmation from the Lord that Isaac had done well so far and would continue to be blessed. Isaac's patience and faith had helped resolve the crisis.

So Isaac built an altar to the Lord, probably sharing with God his relief and gratitude for bringing him through the trials so far. Isaac pitched his tent there, and his servants dug yet another well, but they didn't tell Isaac about it for a few days. At the time, Isaac was too busy preparing for Abimelech's visit. However, was it a visit as a friend or as a foe?

Isaac's Eighth Crisis: Meeting with the Enemy

Isaac must have felt intimidated. Abimelech was coming to see him! Such a powerful man didn't travel without armed guards and advisers (lawyers). Abimelech was accustomed to giving out penalties like water fines and land-use policies (or their equivalent).

Sure enough, the Bible says that Abimelech came along with his personal adviser and the commander of his army. Isaac must have been surprised and a little scared to see him, since Abimelech had basically kicked him out of the city. And what did the army commander intend to do?

Fortunately, Abimelech had a change of heart. "We can plainly see that the LORD is with you," he told Isaac (Genesis 26:28, NLT). Abimelech wanted to swear a peace treaty with Isaac.

Isaac was pleased! He threw a big feast, and they all swore an oath of peace to each other. Afterward, everyone went away and left Isaac to his plenty and his peace.

Finally, Isaac's servants mentioned the good news that they had dug another well and found water, and Isaac named that well "Oath" since it was revealed to him after he took a vow or oath of peace with the Philistines and was left alone to prosper.

Life worked out for Isaac for a number of reasons, which we will explore in the next section. Always mindful of God's promises to him, Isaac sought to be accommodating to the people who were already in the land that God had promised him, moving when they told him to move and re-digging wells they stopped up without retaliation.

Even though he must have been frightened by the approach of Abimelech and his men, questioning their motives, Isaac was open-minded enough to listen to what they had to say. As it turned out, the

Philistines and their king had changed their minds. They could see God in Isaac's life. King Abimelech reminded Isaac that although he had deceived him earlier about Rebekah, Abimelech did right by the couple and protected them. Now, the king desired peace and a non-aggression pact among them. Why did he need a peace treaty needed with a foreigner, an immigrant? Isaac had increased his wealth, power, and territory. Also, Abimelech felt the need to stop the declarations of war (dirt down the wells) and state openly, by signing a peace treaty, that he did not approve of war. Even Abimelech recognized that no matter where Isaac went, he prospered. Politically speaking, Abimelech made a savvy move to align himself with Isaac.

Thus Isaac, who was prepared to fight, found himself hosting a great big party with overnight guests who got up early the next morning, confirmed the peace covenant, and headed for their own homes.

We can see that God validated Isaac's decisions and responses to the crisis by blessing him with even more success than before—Isaac's men found another well that he named "Shebah," meaning "the oath," specifically the oath of peace between Isaac, the king, and the Philistines. This is an example of a fulfilled promise from Proverbs: "When people's lives please the LORD, even their enemies are at peace with them" (Proverbs 16:7, NLT).

"We Get Rid of an Enemy by Getting Rid of Enmity" —Dr. Martin Luther King, Jr.

There are clues to Isaac's character in this series of events. Like his dad before him, Isaac seemed like an obliging guy. In his book *Pursuing the Will of God,*[viii] Pastor Jack Hayford points out how obliging and unselfish Abraham was when, in a situation similar to Isaac's, his servants quarreled with Lot's servants over water, land, herds, and other things valuable for survival in the valley. Abraham told Lot to choose where he wanted to go—to the left or to the right—and he, Abraham, would accommodate him and go the other way so there would be room for everyone. In much the same way, when the Philistines wanted Isaac out of their way, he went peacefully, accommodating their wishes. When they quarreled over a well, he ceded it to them and moved on. When they told him to get out of their land, he went without a murmuring word.

It seems that both Abraham and Isaac had expansive characters; they truly believed that there is plenty of room for all. They didn't get petty and quarrel over territory and wells. They moved on in confidence that the Lord had promised to take care of them.

Isaac's actions may be even greater because he showed grace to people who were not relatives, as Lot had been to Abraham. Most of us try to keep peace with members of our families. Abimelech and the Philistine herdsmen were not of Isaac's family, not of his tribe, not of his faith—they treated him as an enemy.

This story of Isaac offers the foundation of Christianity. Years later, Jesus told us to love our enemies, and Paul enjoined us to understand that in God's eyes there is little difference between people who call upon Him (Romans 10:12, KJV). The era of caring only about our own families, our own tribes, and our own societies was over once Jesus came. We are supposed to care about everyone and seek to live in peace with others, loving our neighbors even if they are different from us—even if our neighbors act like enemies. Isaac was a tremendous example of this Christ-like behavior.

Isaac didn't get mad or try to retaliate against the people who pushed him out and cut off his lifeline of water. There is no record of him taking an angry action. Dr. Martin Luther King, Jr., said, "We get rid of an enemy by getting rid of enmity." Even though some translations say that Isaac named one of the wells "Enmity," it appears that he didn't keep any ill feelings in his heart. Nor does it seem that he judged the Philistines too harshly for their incessant jealousy over his prosperity.

Perhaps Isaac's gracious heart helped bring about the change of heart in Abimelech, who came to pursue peace and friendship. Isaac's attitude made the difference. Perhaps that's how the Philistines saw that he was of God: he didn't return spite for spite, jealousy for jealousy, anger and pettiness for anger and pettiness. He moved on to a place where he perceived there was plenty of room. And when they followed him there, he accommodated them again, moving several times to appease the quarrelsome, jealous people and not fighting them, though he certainly had the resources to do so.

Although the Bible does not give us a time frame between the naming of the "Jealous" well and the one that symbolized an "Oath" of peace, the word "finally" seems to indicate that Isaac may have thought long and hard before digging another well. The constant bickering and conflict could have caused him to shut down his operations and give up, saying, "Every time I dig a well, someone stirs up trouble. I should stop digging them here. This land will never be mine. The Lord's promises aren't going to come true."

But he didn't give up. He didn't wallow in self-pity. He calmly moved on in faith.

A Survival Guide for Your Desert Valley Experience

Our lives are always in transition. For instance, we leave our beds every morning and enter the bathroom to prepare for the day. We leave old careers for new ones. Our children get older, leaving their infant years to become toddlers, school-age children, teenagers, and finally independent adults. We transition from childhood to puberty, from puberty into being parents, through mid-life crises and into old age. We move from place to place and sometimes from state to state. Our jobs may change in nature, locale, and pay scale. Our parents, who took care of us when we were young, grow older and need us to take care of them. We endure the deaths of friends and loved ones.

The only constant in life is change.

Years ago, doctors created a stress scale, noting that any kind of change—even happy ones—bring attendant stresses. Change is the norm, so we have to be prepared for it and learn how to cope with it well. Some great changes wind up being not so good. Some changes that seem awful at first wind up being not so bad. The only sure thing is that change will come, and it will bring some kind of stress with it.

What about times when change is especially challenging? You may change from being healthy to facing a difficult diagnosis. You may change from having a job to being unemployed. You may change from being a happy parent of children to being an unhappy parent of rebellious teenagers. You may change from enjoying a loving, romantic marriage to suffering through one where you can't seem to stop fighting. You may change from being well off to being bankrupt. You may change from being a parent to experiencing the death of a child. You may change from being married to being alone. You may change from having your parents to turn to into being the parent everyone else turns to; you are now the head of the family. You may change from having one job at work to having five—with a pay cut thrown in to boot.

Negative changes can be called a desert or valley or wilderness experience. In the Bible, these terms convey a place of great personal trials, tribulations, and even spiritual warfare. It is no coincidence that Isaac went into the Valley of Gerar, where he had to confront several crises. Throughout human history, valleys have been known to make or break people. For the believer, valleys are supposed to be temporary places that we pass through. David offers this encouragement in Psalm 23: "Even when I walk through the darkest valley, I will not be afraid, for you are close beside me. Your rod and your staff protect and comfort me" (Psalm 23:4, NLT).

Some valley experiences, like a divorce, the loss of a job, or the death of a loved one, last longer than others. We must decide, however, how to respond in the valley. When we are in a valley like Isaac's Valley of Gerar, will we dig our own wells or dig our own graves? Will we bury our heads in the sand and give up, or will we try to start over again and rebuild?

A philosopher once said that we are responsible for everything but the fact that we have responsibility. God gave us responsibility. We must then choose how to use our "response-ability"—our ability to respond—in valley situations. Are we going to be proactive or reactive? Are we going to whine and complain, or are we going to dig a well so we can drink even in the deepest valley of the desert?

For inspiration, we can look to Isaac in the Valley of Gerar. He did not give up. He did not wallow in self-pity. He did not bury his head in the sand. He knew that jealousy, strife, enmity, and envy were at work, and he dealt with them in the following way: "Then Isaac built an altar there and worshiped the LORD. He set up his camp at that place, and his servants dug another well" (Genesis 26:25, NLT). And at that point, King Abimelech came to ask for peace.

When you come to the valley, go to God in prayer, and worship your way through your trials. Don't stop looking for new wells. Don't stop digging. You will be refreshed, even in the deepest valley, the darkest wilderness, or the driest desert.

Finding the Water

One of the most important survival tips for people who are lost is to find water. In fact, every United States soldier is issued a handbook that instructs the GI on how to survive the most horrid conditions, and finding water is always an essential step. As you face a spiritual and emotional valley, sometimes you have to dig out your father's old, stopped-up wells, just like Isaac did. You may have to revisit some of the battles your parents already fought, especially if they left unfinished business. Your parents' reputations may either support you or burden you. Your parents' financial situation may be either a cushion or a curse. You may find yourself saying the same things to your children that your parents said to you—things you vowed would never come out of your lips!

If you overcome in areas where your parents didn't, you will have great victories and great blessings. Of course, the more faithful your parents were, the clearer your way will be to taking advantage of your special inheritances from them. Your parents might have known where the water was, but some enemy—other people, time, or circumstances—stopped up their wells. Dig out those wells and find the water again.

Someone once said, "You've got to slay your own giants." Sometimes Satan won't stop trying to take what is yours, even if it comes through inheritance, until you fight hard for it.

Admittedly, troubling situations can seem deflating, standing over us like a bully and daring us to get up. Sometimes it seems as if the Lord has abandoned us, but in actuality He is saying, "Latch onto my strength, and muster the courage to get up after you are knocked down." We only lose if we refuse to get up again—if we give up.

Isaac refused to give up. He needed the Lord's encouragement, to be sure, and he must have had doubts, but his actions and reactions were godly and controlled. In that way, he found peace.

Just because someone invites you to get into a fight, you don't have to accept the invitation. Isaac didn't. He peaceably went on his way, even when his patience and fears were sorely tried, and in the end, his enemies came after him, telling him how godly he was and asking for peace between them!

That's victory! That's Isaac inheriting the best of his father's character and acting in the same faithful, calm, and peaceable way: willing to share the wealth and willing to take the harder route so that others could be accommodated and happy. These were not the actions of a wimp or a doormat. These were the actions of a man so powerful that others envied him and told him he needed to go before he took them over. Isaac was a gracious and powerful man who lived in peace, even in the valley of the desert.

I'd like to offer a final word about "Jealousy," which was one of the names of the wells and also the reason the Philistines harassed Isaac over his land and water. Jealousy often results from low self-esteem. I've noticed that Christian believers tend to be at one of two extremes when it comes to their self-esteem: high or low (with precious little in between). If you have low self-esteem, you are probably comparing yourself unfavorably with others: Why does that person have so much? Why does every bird in Isaac's flock have a ton of fledglings when mine only have one or two? What's with that guy? He's not much better than me! I'm going to shove some dirt down his well. I'm going to spread gossip, rumors, and put-downs about him.

One cure for jealousy is to realize that there is room for all, as Isaac understood after several desert experiences. Every person has his or her special gift or talent from God. Our business is not to envy others their gifts; our business is to find and develop ours. The world is full of resources—many of them untapped. There are many wells in the world! Imagine a world in which every person was motivated to help others. If people helped one another more, the world's prosperity quotient would soar higher than we could ever believe. There is plenty for all if we believe it, see it, and act on it. Use your gifts to tap into the well of plenty, and help others along the way. You will find, like Isaac, that there is room for all. When you move over and make room for others, you'll be more at peace with them and with yourself too.

We've defined a desert time as a period when it seems like there isn't enough of something in our lives—enough peace, enough love, enough money, enough work. Yet God is a God of abundance, so envy has no place in our hearts. This realization is a leap of faith, telling God that we know He will give us plenty of room and plenty of water and everything else we need. It's also accepting that even a small amount is enough to get us through valleys and deserts and tough times.

Day always follows night. Spring always follows winter. Remember that good times will follow bad ones, as sure as the sun comes up, and put your faith in the idea that the Lord's thoughts toward you are ones of peace, to give you a future and a hope: "'For I know the plans I have for you,' declares the LORD, 'plans to prosper you and not to harm you, plans to give you hope and a future'" (Jeremiah 29:11, NIV). Be assured that there is plenty to go around. You will get through the dry desert valleys and come out into the oases of better times.

When times are tough, build an altar to the Lord, as Isaac did. Soon after, you will find a well.

Peace with our neighbors, peace in our families, prosperity, having others acknowledge that we are blessed by the Lord (as Abimelech did with Isaac)—these are signs of true success and true wealth. Some of it translates into material wealth, because we save time and energy by avoiding the drama that accompanies being out of sync with the Lord and with others.

Conflict, strife, and estrangement take tremendous tolls on our productivity and our thinking. How can a husband and wife come up with a financial plan to pay down the debt and fund a college education if there is no peace between them? How can a body of believers bring in new people if strife, jealousy, power plays, recriminations, and judgment run rife among its members, and how will that church prosper if no one new is joining? The dividends of peace abound; we just don't notice them as we willingly sow discord.

Why should you go into a foreign land? For some people, simply leaving your air-conditioned house to say hello to a neighbor on a summer night is taking a journey to a foreign land. On a practical level, going to a "foreign land" exposes you to new information that can help you overcome your situation. Sometimes a friend tells you about a website that enables a person to make tens of thousands of dollars over a number of years of hard work. Sometimes a neighbor mentions a great summer program for kids that can relieve a young mother during the busiest months at her seasonal work, and she knows that her kids are enjoying constructive, protected activities. Sometimes someone at your kid's baseball game reminds you of the form your child needs at school in order to take the big test that will determine much of his future academic life. People are a great resource, so go out into the "foreign land" of new acquaintances, friends, and activities. It will enrich your life in unexpected ways. Taking even a small step outside your comfort zone will help counteract the "I, me, mine, my family, my tribe, my faith, my church, my ethnic group" thinking that Isaac confronted in the Valley of Gerar, where he learned to get along with his "enemies."

Researchers have found that the most creative people are multicultural, and many have literally spent time in a foreign land. The more open you are to others—the more you believe, as Isaac did, that there is plenty of room for all—the more you will be blessed. As you give your regard, respect, and time to others who may be different from you, you experience greater blessings.

Keep in mind that wealth is relative. There is always someone who has less and always someone who has more. Don't compare yourself, unless it is to try to help the less fortunate through your blessings. If you live in America, you're wealthier than most people in the world and most people in human history. Just having hot, running water is more than a lot of people ever had or ever will have. Consider the blessing of electricity—something we don't notice and appreciate until a storm takes it away for a while! It is a blessing to have a couple of dimes to knock together. Some people in the world do not see a shiny silver dime more than once a month—if then. In some countries, people's annual wages are less than a few dollars in our money. In a world where the majority of people are in want, there is no room to envy other people's wealth.

Let's be grateful for what we have, and we will discover that we have more than enough and more than we need. There's room for all, as Isaac noted. In many ways, abundance is a state of mind. Let's celebrate as Isaac celebrated, knowing that there is room for all and plenty for all.

TAKEAWAYS

- The only constant in life is change. Change and crisis will come. We must adapt patiently and faithfully hold on to God's unchanging hand.
- Isaac gives an example of being accommodating, faithful, friendly, and forgiving in the face of constant changes.
- Even our enemies will become our friends if we banish enmity from our hearts.
- Don't stop digging. Pray and worship the Lord through adversity. You will find a new well that will refresh and sustain your life.
- God is called "More than Enough" or "Plenty," even when we may only see lack, loss, or pain (2 Corinthians 5:7, KJV). Be encouraged; troubles don't last forever.
- There is no need for wells called "Quarrel" and "Jealousy." There is "Plenty of Room for All" in God's abundant world and His Kingdom.

12

DEALING WITH FAMILY MATTERS

Like her mother-in-law before her, Rebekah was barren—the first crisis we explored in Isaac's life. Isaac prayed to the Lord, and Rebekah conceived male twins. In those days, two sons all at once were considered a major blessing. It seems that these two boys were quite a handful from the beginning.

Isaac was forty years old when he married Rebekah (Genesis 25:20, NLT), and he was sixty years old when his sons were born. That is an advanced age to be dealing with rambunctious male twins! On top of that, Jacob and Esau fought all the time. They were even fighting in the womb, leading Rebekah to ask the Lord about it because she could feel them jostling each other.

The Lord said to her, "The sons in your womb will become two nations. From the very beginning, the two nations will be rivals. One nation will be stronger than the other; and your older son will serve your younger son" (Genesis 25:23, NLT).

That must have been interesting news, because in those days, the elder son of a family inherited everything—the land, the flocks, the herds, the money, any dwellings, water rights, and more. The older brother was supposed to take care of his siblings with the money he inherited, but in some cases, the older brothers kept most of it for themselves. For an older brother to serve a younger brother was unheard of. In this hierarchical society, the eldest son was the prince of the home.

Jacob emerged a few seconds after Esau did and was considered the younger son. Yet he was so determined to surpass his brother that he came out clinging to Esau's heel. If they started life this way, we can imagine how competitive they were. Their sibling rivalry was probably exacerbated by the fact that Isaac and Rebekah played favorites. Since Isaac had a taste for wild game, he appreciated Esau, who was good at hunting. Rebekah liked Jacob better, since he hung around at home and was more quiet and reserved.

Still, Jacob was clever. One day when Esau returned home, ravenous from hunting, Jacob tricked him. He offered him some savory stew to eat if Esau would renounce his position as the elder son, which was Esau's birthright. This would effectively put Jacob in the position of the elder son, with all the attendant rights and privileges, including the right to inherit all that Isaac had. Esau took him up on the bargain! That stew smelled so good and he was so hungry from hunting that he sold his birthright to Jacob. Jacob also tricked his father into giving him the blessing of the elder son, which meant that Jacob, not Esau, inherited all the blessings of Abraham, including "May many nations become your servants" (Genesis 27:29, NLT); and he, not Esau, became the forefather of the Jewish people. We say "Abraham, Isaac, and Jacob," not "Abraham, Isaac, and Esau."

Step by clever step, Jacob took over the right to be the progenitor of Israel. He won the birthright, he won the battle with the angel, he won over his jealous brother, he won himself a great wife (Rachel), and his descendants became the lineage of the nation of Israel and the Messiah.

In part, this happened because Esau married the wrong woman, or women, bringing great grief to Isaac.

Isaac's Ninth Crisis: Unhealthy Pairings

Earlier, we considered the fact that we may have to revisit some of the battles our parents fought, just as Isaac had to re-dig his father's wells. There may be a lot to overcome in a person's relationship with his or her parents. Intergenerational conflicts in families are common. We've all heard the mother-in-law jokes! Sometimes your children, like Isaac's son Esau, will do things that hurt and upset you. In Isaac's case, Esau broke his parents' hearts by marrying two Hittite women. "And they were a grief of mind to Isaac and Rebekah" (Genesis 26:35, NKJV).

If you are a parent, you probably know what "grief of mind" is. When our children do things we disapprove of or when they experience life's inevitable blows, we suffer "grief of mind." Looking at our own parents, we can probably see plenty of ways we caused them "grief of mind," or we remember things that would have caused them grief of mind had they known about them at the time!

We know that Isaac had an expansive mind. He didn't easily shut out other people who were different from him; he welcomed them as friends if they wanted to live in peace with him. But Esau married "heathen" women. They were not just women of a different faith; they had no faith at all. The Bible doesn't say exactly how and why these women were a source of grief for Isaac and Rebekah, but it might have been their lack of faith. "Can two walk together, except they be agreed" (Amos 3:3, KJV)?

What we do see in this story is that, in spite of the fact that Esau made poor marital choices, Isaac still wanted to bless him with the inheritance of God. What a forgiving, forbearing father Isaac was! He accepted Esau as his heir and favored elder son even though Esau did something many faithful and loving parents would struggle with—married someone outside the faith, or from another neighborhood, or from another tribe or group.

As parents, we can truly discover the heart of God when our children do things that go against the values we hoped they would make their own. In the Garden of Eden, God faced the horrific grief of finding that His children had eaten from the forbidden tree and affected human history, introducing sin into the world. Parents whose children (of whatever age) go against their values get to know the heart of God well. The fact that God sent Jesus to redeem the children of fallen Adam becomes an even greater sign of grace and mercy when, as parents, we experience heartbreak from our own children and wonder how to help them redeem their lives.

The parent whose kid gets in trouble at school feels humiliation and pain. The parent who has to answer a call from the police station knows the agony of God. The parents whose kids can't make good grades, whose daughter gets pregnant in high school, whose son uses drugs or gets picked up for drunk driving, whose kids treat them disrespectfully are well acquainted with grief of mind.

We grieve when our children do things that have bad consequences; we also grieve when their good efforts result in failure or ridicule. Even if our children are model children (in fact, especially if they are), we grieve when they are mocked at school. We wonder why they cannot be good and also popular, why they have to suffer for standing up for the values we cherish. We wonder why, when our adult children are excellent employees, they don't get a promotion or a raise while others do.

We wonder why a special someone of the opposite sex can't see our child as the beautiful and good human being that we know him or her to be.

We grieve when our children can't find a job commensurate with their abilities. We grieve when our children face the incidents and accidents of life. We grieve whether their problems stem from themselves or from an evil world that seems to be out to get anyone who tries to be righteous.

Raising young children to adulthood is challenging. But as they mature, they are able to make even more decisions that hurt us, and the consequences are steeper for both children and parents. What if your son or daughter is thirty years old and still playing video games in the living room because he or she quit the latest fast food job while you struggle to make ends meet? What if your grown-up son or daughter's spouse gets a job on the other side of the continent, and they move there, taking your grandchildren to a place you won't often be able to visit? What if, overly stressed from their many responsibilities, your grown-up children are unable to help you when you grow old and are in need of them?[

There are hundreds of ways for children to fail parents and for parents to fail children. In particular in the life of Isaac, his son Esau's choice of wives "made life miserable for Isaac and Rebekah" (Genesis 26:35, NLT). Yet the life of Isaac also provides us with a key for how to cope when our children let us down.

Isaac was forgiving. He still wanted to bless Esau with everything he had. Isaac sent Esau to hunt him up a nice, savory meal before he blessed him (Genesis 27:4, NLT). While Esau was away, Rebekah and Jacob connived to trick Isaac into giving Jacob the blessing of the older son. Rebekah and Jacob prepared a savory meal for Isaac and dressed Jacob to resemble Esau. By the time Esau returned from hunting, Isaac had already transferred God's great family blessings to Jacob. Realizing what he had done, Isaac also knew that he could not take it back. He knew that Esau would live a difficult and violent life, much like Cain in the first family. And, just like Cain, Esau was so jealous of his brother's blessings that he wanted to kill him. He vowed to do so as soon as Isaac died.

We can imagine Rebekah's fear at this point. What if your children's sibling rivalry became so great that one wanted to kill the other? Isaac's household could not have been happy at that point.

Rebekah went to Isaac and said that she didn't want Jacob to repeat Esau's mistake by marrying Canaanite women from the area. She asked if Isaac could send Jacob away to her relatives to find a woman to wed. Isaac agreed, and Jacob went off to safety from Esau's wrath.

It was only then that Esau realized his parents weren't happy about his marriages. What a failure to communicate! Apparently, Isaac had withheld his feelings about Esau's choices. Isaac was stoic, however, and still ready to bless his sons. In fact, when Jacob set off for Haran to find a wife (and escape Esau), Isaac confirmed that Jacob would receive "the blessing of Abraham," which included all the land and enough descendants to become a "community of peoples" (Genesis 28:3).

As it turned out, Jacob found a suitable wife (two, in fact), earned himself a fortune, prospered, and became the father of the bloodlines of Israel, leading right to the Messiah. He also later reconciled with Esau. Peace returned to the family that was blessed by rambunctious, feisty twins and destined to affect whole nations.

We deal with our children throughout their rambunctious childhood years. We deal with them during the in-between years of puberty and adolescence, which may be fraught with difficulties. We deal with them into young adulthood and adulthood. All along the way, we need to forgive them for their shortcomings. We need to be like Isaac, who was forgiving and willing to pass on his inheritance of blessings even when Esau displeased him mightily.

Our Heavenly Father does this for us. We're His children, and we let Him down every day. The sharp word to our spouses, the skipping of prayer and worship because we are "too tired" from work, the "minor" cheating on financial forms that we think no one will notice, the dislike we harbor in our hearts for a coworker or member of our fellowship year after year, keeping the grudge and resentment alive and well—these are everyday examples of how we let God down. And these are the lesser transgressions!

When it comes to raising errant children, God is truly the king! God has suffered along with humanity since the beginning. God has borne our sorrows and our burdens and grieved for how blind we sometimes are. God sent His Son, Jesus, as a redeemer and example. God's grace has been poured out through the ages for any child who knocks on the door, who seeks, and who asks (Revelation 3:20). He bears the burden of our sins and, like a loving parent, embraces us fully whenever we make a gesture to return to Him.

We must learn to be wise parents like God. Wise parents know when to stand back and not take too many of the children's consequences into their own hearts, especially if the children are adults. God gave everyone free will. Beyond a certain point, there is little we can do to persuade and influence our children to adopt our ways and accept Jesus as Lord. We can pray. We can love. We can forgive. We can try to accept them as they are. If circumstances get too bad, we can institute "tough love" or "loving detachment" where we let our children experience the full consequences of their choices, unshielded by us.

Like Isaac, who reflected the nature of God, we too can still embrace and bless our children even when they don't embrace our values. Like God, we can respond favorably and with an outpouring of love when our children embrace the values we treasure.

How much we should help, how much we should say, how much we should intervene—these are delicate balances that require great wisdom and great love. Isaac was apparently so careful about how he spoke to his children that Esau didn't even know his wives were making his parents miserable.

Parenting well is one of the hardest tasks a person can undertake. As parents, we must forgive ourselves if we make mistakes along the way; we should confess them to the Lord, repent, and do everything we can to make up for them. God will restore the lost years, just as He worked to restore Isaac's family and keep them in position as the family of faith that would affect Israel and its messianic destiny.

Hopefully, we can be parents like Isaac—ready to bless our errant sons or daughters with everything we have, no matter what. In Isaac's case, through the machinations of Jacob and Rebekah, Jacob wound up getting the blessing that belonged to his brother. Esau was justifiably angry with Jacob, but he certainly could not complain that his father treated him poorly and didn't love him.

Parental love is redemptive love; it wants what is best for the child (no matter how old the child is). God's rules and regulations of life are for our benefit, so that we can experience healthy, happy, spiritually full, and fulfilling lives. We want what is best for our children so that they suffer less and fulfill their purpose more. We pray for them and counsel them as well as we can and in the ways they allow us to. We guide and help as much as possible without compromising ourselves. We love our children with the love of

God—and we understand more about God's heart as the ultimate Parent.

From what we can see in the story of Isaac, he experienced a parent's joy and a parent's grief. Isaac worried about his children. Esau said he was going to kill Jacob. Would he succeed? I assume that Isaac wondered how Jacob was doing in Haran when he was sent away from home. Even though Isaac and Rebekah had put up with the heathen women all this time, they still tried to be accommodating when their son, Esau, married one. With the help of Isaac's steadfast love, his sons prospered and grew wealthy. Eventually, the brothers reconciled after their terrible quarrel, and they retained the blessing from God that would create nations out of their lineage. All in all, they were a successful family, and when Isaac died, his sons, Jacob and Esau, buried him with respect and love. Isaac lived for 180 years and died peacefully, "gathered to his people" (Genesis 35:29, KJV). Abraham, Isaac, and Jacob are considered the fathers of Christianity because they stood on the promises of God. The fulfilled promises of God ultimately led to the salvation of the world, through their lineage, with the birth, death and resurrection of Jesus Christ.

TAKEAWAYS

- Isaac and Rebekah faced difficult trials involving their unruly children, Jacob and Esau. Your children will test your love.
- Isaac showed that he was a forbearing, long-suffering, and forgiving father.
- Parental love is redemptive love; it wants what is best for the child. God is like a Parent with us.
- Jacob inherited God's blessing on the family of Abraham and became the father of the twelve tribes of Israel.
- The Abraham-Isaac-Jacob trio of great fathers was recognized in God's eyes. Centuries later, even Jesus recognized a well that Jacob had built as a forefather of Israel.

13
BECOMING A MASTER DRILLER

In this chapter, we discuss how to become a master driller of wells in our lives. In this case, a well is a place where you can go for spiritual sustenance—a place where you can refresh your thirst and gain the strength, wisdom, and support to pick up and go on in your journey of life.

There are many ways to dig wells; the first may surprise you. You can dig a well by resting!

A master of anything knows when to pause. Many times when we face life's challenges, we act without thinking them through properly or giving ourselves adequate care and rest. Yet sometimes during a period of rest, the answers crystallize, peace comes, and we can hear the voice of God. After all, He once said, "Be still and know that I am God" (Psalm 46:10). He told us to be still sometimes so that our spirits will be at peace enough to receive guidance.

Consider the fact that many great discoveries have come when a person was at rest. The most famous is probably when Sir Isaac Newton decided to take a nap under a tree, got struck on the head with an apple, and worked out the law of gravity.

Not every guy would have come up with that. Newton is considered the greatest scientist of all time—the master of them all. He taught, discovered, wrote, and has been highly respected in his field to this day. The man was a master of physics.

Because Newton did his homework, an understanding of gravity came to him in a moment of rest, and he was able to articulate and apply it. Newton had filled his mind with information and knowledge; he had puzzled over the questions quite a bit. But in a moment of repose, when Newton let it all go and got busy resting, the answer became crystal clear.

Many discoveries, scientific and otherwise, come when the mind is at rest. We experience the so-called "Eureka!" moment when everything comes together in perfect harmony after weeks, months, and years of effort.

To become a master driller, you need to put forth the effort, just as Newton did. You need to know your field; you need to have traveled down all kinds of avenues within it, worked hard, and gained understanding. You have to try your best. Yet you also have to know how to take moments of repose in the Lord.

Isaac rested. He had moved several times during the trouble in Gerar. After that, Isaac rested. He found a third well that everyone left alone, named it "Plenty of Room for All," and took a little rest. And the Lord appeared to him that night (Genesis 26:24).

What are we usually doing at night? Resting. Our muscles relax, our minds travel toward dreamland, and we let down some of our defenses and give up the stresses of the day. At this time of day, the Lord "appeared" to Isaac and renewed the promises He had made to Abraham: "I am the God of your father, Abraham. Do not be afraid, for I am with you and will bless you. I will multiply your descendants, and they will become a great nation. I will do this because of my promise to Abraham, my servant" (Genesis 26:24, NLT).

It is said that there is a time between waking and sleeping when we sometimes receive the most vivid spiritual messages. Often, in the Bible, the Lord appears to people in a dream or through a dream-like state, close to the time of actual sleep.

If Isaac had been running around, stressing out about wells and nasty herdsman, pacing the floor, and grinding his teeth over Abimelech, it is unlikely that he would have had room in his consciousness for God to speak to him. Yet because Isaac had let go of so much (his home in Gerar city, his water rights twice, etc.), God could come and speak to him of a beautiful future as he rested at Beersheba.

In a similar way, when Jacob, Isaac's son, slept, God showed him a "ladder" or a "staircase" to Heaven. In his dream, Jacob saw angels running up and down on the staircase between Heaven and earth, and the Lord appeared, renewing the promise of many descendants, the land, and the power of influence over all peoples of the earth. "I am with you," the Lord promised Jacob, "and I will protect you wherever you go. One day I will bring you back to this land. I will not leave you until I have finished giving you everything I have promised you" (Genesis 28:15, NLT). During this time of rest, the Lord reassured Jacob that all would be well.

We need to create spaces and pockets of time when the Lord can speak to us. This may be first thing in the morning, before the world is up and the pace of life runs away with us and the noises of activity fill our ears. It could be before bedtime. But choose a time to "steal away to Jesus." It is a time when you can be alone with the Lord without distractions and lean on the everlasting arms. We can rest in the Lord, knowing that He is taking care of everything now that we have given our best effort. The harvest is up to God.

Get Busy Resting!

One of the most wonderful things the Lord offers us is peace. Have you ever had a heart full of troubles, turned to the Lord in prayer, and then found that so many of them seemed to melt away? Maybe they didn't literally disappear from your everyday reality, but your heart was at peace about them. You truly felt that everything would be all right because you gave your troubles to the Lord.

Jesus said, "Come to me, all of you who are weary and carry heavy burdens, and I will give you rest" (Matthew 11:28, NLT). Paul and Timothy urge us to come before the altar, make our petitions known, and be filled with "the peace of God, which passeth all understanding" (Philippians 4:7, KJV). That peace provides the greatest rest for our souls.

How do we rest in the Lord? In Psalm 37, King David tells us not to fret. "Trust in the LORD, and do good," he said (Psalm 37:3, NLT), because evil people will not prosper in the long term. Eventually, the righteous will be taken care of. If you commit yourself to Jesus Christ, entrusting Him with your past, present, and future, you don't need to worry.

A bumper sticker says, "Why worry when you can pray?" Why, indeed?

Many times we fret and become agitated about things over which we have no control. "Rest in the LORD," King David tells us (Psalm 37:7, KJV), and wait patiently for Him. "Fret not," he says, (Psalm 37:1, KJV), for "the meek shall inherit the earth; and shall delight themselves in the abundance of peace" (verse 11).

Peace and rest in God come when you and I give our troubles to Him and let Him work on them.

At the same time, when we have a heart full of trouble, it is often hard to turn to the Lord. We try to pray, but we can't. Our minds and hearts fill with anguish, dread, and anxiety. Maybe we even blame the Lord for the bad things that happen around us or in our lives, and we find it hard to talk to Him. Still, speaking our feelings and thoughts in prayer is the best policy. God is strong enough to take it when we confess, "Lord, some things went wrong, and I'm even a little angry at You. I thought my family would be protected. I thought You had us covered, and look what happened. I know Your thoughts toward us are thoughts of peace, but I am having these feelings. Please help me find my way through." God will help you understand and accept that bad things happen because of human free will, sin, and the evil one, never because of Him.

God will lead you out of your desert experience victoriously. But you still have to walk through the desert to get out of it. When I was deployed to Saudi Arabia for "Operation Desert Storm," my wife (then fiancée) sent sermon tapes to encourage me. One sermon was

"Lord, Get Me Out of This and Get This Out of Me," by Reverend Regina Harris. Her sermon title had a twofold meaning for me. One was the obvious literal meaning of me getting physically out of the desert alive. The other was a spiritual meaning of calming my mind. I needed to rest. I needed to rest in God. I needed the peace of God in the middle of a desert conflict. While I was in my literal desert, I drew closer to the Lord as did many other soldiers in my unit. There were some who abandoned Jesus while under pressure, however, and they blamed God for their plight. We all have a choice to make in the middle of a desert experience. That choice should be easy. But when we are in the thick of it, the solution is not so easily apparent. For me, the choice was "to live is Christ [His life in me], and to die is gain [the gain of the glory of eternity]" (Philippians 1:21, AMP). I was under orders to stay in the desert, and I could not leave until my mission was complete.

If you are in your own desert right now, rest assured that God already has made provisions for you until you are able to leave that difficult place. Remember that there are wells to refresh you and oases where you can rest until you are able to walk out of the desert victoriously.

A teenage boy had gotten his driver's license and a part-time job. He needed the family car to get to and from his job, and his parents let him borrow it when they could. But when they needed the car, they either dropped him off at work or advised him to take the bus, which the boy hated to do. One cold and rainy day, the parents had to work, so they could not take their son to his job. They suggested that he take the bus, but he said that if he couldn't use the car, he would walk to work—over two miles. He was resentful that he had put a full tank of gas in the car and would not be able to use it. The parents felt bad, but they knew that walking in the cold rain was the boy's choice.

Still, the thought of the boy walking two miles in poor weather bothered the mother's heart. It was not easy to stand strong, and it upset her that her teenager, with the usual reasoning powers of the adolescent, was clearly angry about the situation. She prayed and decided to rest in the Lord. She put it in God's hands and peacefully went about her way. She said nothing more to her son and let her dictum about the car stand.

Later, the boy announced that he could get a ride from a friend. In fact, he thanked his parents for standing strong, since it forced him to be resourceful. Plus, he was going to get time to spend with his friend! Peace was restored. Everyone was happier with the situation than if the parents had caved in and let the boy have his way. Even the teenage boy ended up happy and proud. The family actually remembered the incident as a time when dissension was avoided and happiness took its place because the parents stood still and rested in God, trusting Him to work it out.

Of course, human beings have to make every effort, because God does help those who help themselves. The Lord wants strong and capable people, and many of our trials are designed to help us become just that. Yet there are times when we need to surrender control to God. The Lord does it better, anyway.

This does not mean surrendering responsibility. It does not mean showing up in prayer with a long to-do list for God. It means that, when you sense that you need to let go, you allow God to take over. It's a matter of humility. There are times when we have to admit that we haven't got the smarts, the guts, or the wherewithal to oversee something, and that we can't control everything—especially other human beings. That's when it's time to give the Lord the glory by letting Him work.

God is a master at dealing with people and their free will. God invented free will, after all. If even the Lord can't control other people, then we certainly can't. What we can do is ask Him to penetrate people's consciousness so that they may be moved to do the right thing. These are powerful prayers. When things go wrong, we have to know that it was because of people's own choices and the devil's work. We can be assured that God is doing all He can to help us.

If you're mad at someone and you want God to rain down fire on his or her head, try praying instead that the person's conscience is awakened. Pray for the person to be saved by God's grace and live as a true child of the King. Then leave everything, including judgment, in God's hands. Leave the work in His hands. Peacefully go about your business. You've done your part; you can bet that He'll do his. He wants that person to improve too.

It may take a little time. If you are in constant contact with an irritating person at home or at work, you may need to pray more than once about the situation. At the very least, even if the person's free will is causing him or her to act stubbornly and not change, the Lord will change you. Because you are willing to go to Him in prayer, He will change your heart so that you are able to bear the situation, to experience happiness in spite of what's happening, and to find creative ways to cope with life.

Once you turn a situation over to God, rest in the Lord. He'll take care of it. By no means does this mean we treat God like an ATM machine or a short-order cook. Instead, it means nurturing a deep relationship with God so that we are in His will and able to make our requests respectfully and gratefully known (Philippians 4:6, KJV), lining up our requests to the will of God (Matthew 6:10).

It is important to thank the Lord—profusely—for all that He does. He enjoys praise as well. This is a way to give back to God for answered prayers and all the benefits He gives. Some people count five things to be thankful for each night before going to sleep as a way of grounding themselves in gratitude.

Even if a prayer does not appear to have been answered, that doesn't mean God did not hear your petition. Maybe people's free will blocked His will. Maybe it wouldn't have been good for you, and as a good parent, God had to stand firm and deny your request. At the same time, just having air to breathe, water to drink, food to eat, and life itself are reasons to thank God every day. Gratitude draws God closer. Gratitude also brings us peace and rest, because it makes us realize how much God is there and how much He is doing for us every moment of every day. Being grateful is resting in the Lord.

Perhaps the words of "Leaning on the Everlasting Arms" by Elisha A. Hoffman can help us understand placing ourselves in the arms of God:

> What a fellowship, what a joy divine,
> Leaning on the everlasting arms;
> What a blessedness, what a peace is mine,
> Leaning on the everlasting arms.
>
> (Refrain)
> Leaning, leaning, safe and secure from all alarms;
> Leaning, leaning, leaning on the everlasting arms.
>
> Oh, how sweet to walk in this pilgrim way,
> Leaning on the everlasting arms;
> Oh, how bright the path grows from day to day,
> Leaning on the everlasting arms.
>
> What have I to dread, what have I to fear,
> Leaning on the everlasting arms?
> I have blessed peace with my Lord so near,
> Leaning on the everlasting arms.

What have we to fear, what have we to dread, when we are "leaning on the everlasting arms"? There we are "safe and secure from all alarms" and at peace, because we know that God is faithful and a present help in time of trouble (Psalm 46:1, KJV). Resting allows us to drink from the well of God's everlasting love and His present grace.

How to Develop Unshakeable Confidence

A popular commercial for Gatorade asked, "Is it in you?" Is trust in the Lord "in you"? Do you trust God enough to rest in Him and have confidence that things will turn out well if you leave them to Him? If trust is in you, you are becoming a master driller of life-giving wells, a person who will have a well-watered life. When praying and reading the Word become part of our lifestyle, then we can walk in confidence because communion with God will be as natural as breathing. When that happens, it's not hard to turn to the Lord quickly in times of need because the lines of communication are already open. If we are used to studying, praying, thanking, and praising, then we're also used to listening to the Lord and speaking to Him. We're master drillers. We know where the water is, and we know how to get to it.

One office manager says he became so adept at prayer that he could close his eyes briefly and breathe a quick prayer just before pushing open his boss's door to go in for a talk. He prayed that the talk would go well, and it did. That was because this particular man started each day with prayer, Bible study, and seeking and basking in the presence of the Lord. He was "prayed up" every day, from the moment he arose from bed. He had God on "speed dial" because he had put in the time, care, effort, and work to connect with God each day. He kept in close touch, so when time was at a premium, he could pray quickly and hear from God.

Many of us feel awkward talking with a stranger. Don't be a stranger to God. The more you talk with the Lord, the more you will want to talk with Him, and the more you will notice how much He is doing for you every day and in every way. You will become familiar with the Lord and it will be easier to go to Him, even when your heart and mind are tangled up in difficulties.

One of the most common pieces of advice given to parents of teenagers is to keep the lines of communication open. Therapists and experts recommend talking to your teen about anything and everything. Not every talk has to be a heavy one about major issues like drugs, sex, and violence. Chatting about the teenagers' favorite TV show or hobby, current events, a movie you both saw, or a nice interchange you had with the neighbors is important too; it makes communication more fluid between you. When you are comfortable talking with a person, it is easier to discuss more serious issues because you have good patterns to follow.

Likewise, we should talk to God often, and not just about major issues or problems. We should stay in close touch. Scientific researchers have shown that being grateful lifts depression. It's better than Prozac! Gratitude is a natural, easily accessible way to lift your spirits and keep you in touch with the Almighty, and it's available to every person. If you aren't in the habit of giving thanks to God, you can start with five things each day, counting them on one hand as soon as you get up in the morning or right before you go to bed.

If you start thanking the Lord, you'll find more and more things to be grateful for. In addition to the air we breathe, the water we drink and bathe in, and the food we consume, we live in an era when doctors understand germ theory. Many mothers and children died before the end of the nineteenth century simply because doctors did not wash their hands before delivering babies. Doctors did not know about the tiny "germs" that were literally killing thousands of women and their children. The fact that we have a medicine called penicillin to kill germs may have already saved your life or the lives of your children many times over. There is much to be grateful for in everyday life.

God created and coordinated a solar system so perfect that the planets move around in the universe and never smack into one another. We are safe and sound on earth. If we think about all of God's beneficences, we have more to thank Him for than we have time to thank Him! As you become more limber in offering gratitude, you can increase your "five finger exercise" to include the other hand, increasing your list to ten things you are grateful for every day. In time, you might want to keep a gratitude journal to name what you are grateful for each day, working your way up to dozens of things to list. This is a powerful antidote for depression, which is an epidemic in our society. If we had an epidemic of gratitude, it seems that many of society's problems would start to disappear.

Rooting your heart and mind in God means that your day will bear good fruits; if it's a tough day, you know that you will weather it.

You can have unshakeable confidence that God will walk with you through it.

Psalm 118:8 says, "It is better to take refuge in the LORD than to trust in man. It is better to take refuge in the LORD than to trust in princes" (NLT). God promises us to guide us in Proverbs 3:5-6: "Trust in the LORD with all your heart; do not depend on your own understanding. Seek his will in all you do, and he will show you which path to take" (NLT). Ezekiel 28:26 speaks of God's protection: "and they shall dwell safely therein, and shall build houses, and plant vineyards; yea, they shall dwell with confidence" (KJV).

According to the promise in Ephesians 3:12, we can have complete, unshakeable confidence: "Because of Christ and our faith in Him, we can now come boldly and confidently into God's presence" (NLT). Hebrews 3:6 says we can be confident that "Christ, as the Son, is in charge of God's entire house. And we are God's house, if we keep our courage and remain confident in our hope in Christ" (NLT). Is Christ in charge of your house? If he is, you have nothing to fear.

Prayer is a bottomless well from which to drink sweet water. Peace and gratitude are also deep wells full of delicious, refreshing water. These are ways to rest in the Lord and build unshakable confidence in God. So take a breath and let go of the concerns of the world, knowing that God will never leave us or forsake us (Hebrews 13:5, KJV), and, in the end, everything will be all right.

A master driller is confident in the Lord. A master driller knows when to work and when to rest and when to leave the results up to

God. A master driller knows that he or she is actually just the instrument of the true Master Driller—the Source and Creator of all wells of life-giving waters, both physical and metaphysical.

TAKEAWAYS

- We need to find the time to put aside our "busyness" and rest in the Lord. Great things can happen during a period of rest.
- Accept the fact that God is in charge. He can take care of things. He can handle it.
- This does not mean we sit and wait and do nothing. It means that we are to do what we know to do (James 4:17) and leave the rest up to God.
- Prayer, peace, and gratitude are ways to rest in the Lord and build unshakable confidence in God.
- God will lead you out of your desert experience victoriously. But you still have to walk through the desert to get out of it.

14
SAME RAIN, DIFFERENT UMBRELLA

While in the military, I was deployed to Saudi Arabia for "Operation Desert Storm." Like most people, I never lived in a desert area and had no clue about desert life. I was in for a crash course of real desert life, up close and personal. We landed in the dead of night. It was pitch black and ice cold. The cold felt like razors cutting my face, and my body ached all over. Then came daybreak, and by high noon the heat was unbearable, especially with all the gear I had to wear. Myth #1: There is little to no rainfall in the desert. That is partially true. It doesn't just rain in the desert; it floods because the water doesn't soak into the sand. We had a swimming pool in no time. Myth #2: There isn't any life in the desert. That is partially true. It is not life as we are accustomed to seeing. But everything in the desert is built to survive. That means the animals are nocturnal and poisonous, with a thick hide and camouflage so you can't see them. What did I do in such a place? I did what I was trained to do. I survived. I adapted. I learned to bloom where I was planted.

The right amount of rain can be life giving, while too much rain can be devastating. Rain can be refreshing, or it can symbolize gloominess. While in the desert of Saudi Arabia, I experienced both. I was glad to see the rain, but I was concerned at the same time. An old saying teaches that "into each life a little rain must fall."

No one has it good all the time, no one has a perfectly untroubled life, and no one has it made. This truth hit hard for a New York City chauffeur. He picked up a family from their swanky apartment overlooking Central Park. They were, as the expression goes, filthy rich.

Yet when the family got in the car, the driver noticed that they called one another the worst kinds of names, words that would never be allowed in his humble house. And why? It was because the teenage daughter forgot her cell phone and left it somewhere in the swanky, beautifully appointed apartment upstairs. Finally, they got the doorman of the building to get it for her, and they settled down grumpily after the delay, the mutual accusations, and the name-calling.

While not all rich families are awful and not all poor families are happy, the wisdom of Proverbs still came to the chauffeur's mind: "Better a dry crust eaten in peace than a house filled with feasting—and conflict" (Proverbs 17:1, NLT). This doesn't mean that we can't enjoy the benefits of money. It means that a little rain must fall into each life; no one is immune to suffering, no matter how rich they may be.

We all forget our cell phones sometimes. Our hard drives crash. We get a notice from the bank that a check bounced. The car has a flat tire. The washing machine breaks down. The list could go on and on. Every day, we face the rain clouds of stresses and strains. If you've had one entirely perfect day in your life, you are lucky. And, even if you do have such a great day, you may be sure that the next day will bring some kind of frustration with it.

The rain comes in big and small storms, and it falls on *everyone*, rich and poor, male and female, city and country dwellers, old and young. What do you do when something "minor" happens, like your hard drive crashes or you leave your cell phone behind? At such times, your true character—and the opportunity to build a new one—comes out.

Matthew 5:45 says that the Lord makes His sun to rise on the evil and on the good, and He sends rain on the just and the unjust. A cigarette-smoking, tough old grandmother took over rearing her four grandchildren because her son and his wife split up over an alcohol problem. She said to my editor, "Everyone gets his or her part of the action." That is, everyone must face his or her own suffering.

The same rain falls on the believer and the unbeliever alike, but believers live under a different umbrella in a house that rests on a solid rock foundation, which is Christ Himself. The world turns to other things—drugs, alcohol, mindless entertainment, meaningless sex, pornography. deafening and soul-deadening music—to try soothe their troubles away. They look for anything that will dull the pain and take their minds off their difficulties. Yet believers have the Comforter who will never leave us or forsake us. Even in tough times, we can have great peace. We can find answers. We can learn lessons. We can gain something of value. For believers, life's rainstorms simply mean that our wells are filling up with life-giving water!

One church acquaintance asked the Lord why he was having so many financial difficulties. Every time he started to pull ahead, something bad happened and he wound up behind again. He'd been a rich man and the envy of his friends, but now his Armani suits showed signs of wear because he could no longer replace them constantly.

Finally, he turned to the Lord, and the answer came during a sermon about the Beatitudes: "Blessed are the meek, for they shall inherit the earth" (Matthew 5:5). Deep in his heart, the man realized that he had not been poor in spirit. He had been arrogant about his wealth, thinking himself better than others, even better than his brothers and sisters in Christ. He realized that God was using the great rod of suffering through financial difficulties to teach him humility. He was grateful then, and he realized how little material goods meant. Instead, he was to store up treasures in Heaven, where they can't be corrupted or torn or frayed (Matthew 6:19-20).

What to Do when It's Sunny

As surely as rain will come, sunshine will light up your life too. There will be happy days, even blissful ones—perfect times with your children, wonderful holidays with family and friends, a raise or promotion, a new house, the merciful news that a growth in your body is benign. The sun will shine. What, if anything, should you do during sunny times besides bask in the warmth of the light?

Sunny times are not opportunities to consider yourself better than others who are less fortunate. They are times to be especially grateful and humble. They are times to give more—more tithes, more time, more sympathy—and to remember when the rain has come in your life in the past so that you don't get too proud. Give more, do more, and express your gratitude to God without being arrogant about it. Jesus talked about people who thank God that they are righteous, not like "those sinners over there" (Luke 18:9-14). Don't assume that your good fortune happens because you are great. It happens because *God* is great.

It is inspiring to think of people like Bill Gates, who has made a fortune that no man could spend in one lifetime. He has billions of dollars. He's consistently listed in financial magazines as the richest or the second richest man in the entire world. He has more money than he knows how to spend, and that's after taking care of all his children for the rest of their lives. The financial sun is definitely shining on Bill Gates. So what should he do?

Bill Gates and his wife decided to set up a foundation in order to help people. He has single-handedly funded medical nonprofits to virtually wipe out polio in India, the second most populous country in the world. India is so vast that it is considered a subcontinent. What kind of prayer must Gates pray at night? "Lord, I wiped out the devastating disease of polio for about one-seventh of the world's population today. I hope this pleases You. Thank You that I could do this. I pray that Your Indian children will be blessed through my efforts, and I am grateful to be able to do this for them."

Bill Gates has started a "billionaires' club" where he invites the billionaires of the world to donate half of their money to charitable causes. He and Warren Buffet have worked together to convince the fabulously wealthy that they have more money than they or their descendants will ever need. They urge these people to invest half their fortunes and their own time and interest in helping others for whom the sun isn't shining right now. Bill and Melinda Gates have testified that their charity work is the most exciting work they have ever done and that the feeling of being able to help people in a substantial way is priceless.

In short, if the sun is shining on you, maybe you can give or lend an umbrella to someone who is standing in the rain. You likely won't be able to give the amount that Bill Gates gives, but you can give what you have. You will have peace and internal rewards, and the sun will either keep shining on you, or you will find that, when the rain does come, you've got plenty of people offering you umbrellas in return. They will remember the time you sheltered them from the rain by sharing or lending your umbrella.

"Whoever gives to the poor will lack nothing, but those who close their eyes to poverty will be cursed," says Proverbs 28:27 (NLT). Psalm 37:25 says, "Once I was young, and now I am old. Yet I have never seen the godly abandoned or their children begging for bread" (NLT). If the sun is shining on you, it is important not to forget those who are standing in the rain.

What to Do when It Rains in Your Life

When you face trials or difficulties, examine your life. What attitudes or actions might have incurred God's displeasure? God is not solely the God of wrath depicted in the Old Testament; the coming of Christ proves that. God has shown us His heart, and we know that He suffers with us, and He wants the best for us. Still, like any parent, He can't completely protect us from all the consequences of our errors. Sometimes we need to learn certain lessons, and God has to let us learn them the hard way if we haven't learned them any other way.

If you cannot find any fault in yourself, then perhaps someone in your family has made mistakes, and you are paying the price. Sometimes we suffer because of others' mistakes. This is not a chance for us to ascribe blame or find fault; it is an opportunity for us to try to find out how to correct errors and get right with God.

We can ask God to tell us what we've done wrong or how we've been in the wrong and how to make restitution. We can also understand that sometimes we suffer from the mistakes of others who are misguided. As His children, we must trust that, in the comforting words of Dr. A. R. Bernard, everything that happens in our lives is "either God-sent or God-used" (see Romans 8:28). In some cases, answers to the question "Why?" are hard to find. The last thing we should do, though, is blame God. He is always doing His best to supply all of His children with a future and a hope that we can rely on. Sometimes humankind's free will and the work of the devil result in terrible storms. Sometimes others' selfishness or withholding cause the rain, and although God can persuade people to change, He cannot violate their free will.

When the answer to "Why?" is hard to find, it is best to put our heads down, persevere, and place our faith in the Lord to see us through and to bring good out of the storm.

When Rain Turns into Floods

We've seen or heard of the powerful devastation caused by floods. Homes are destroyed and lives are lost as the torrential water is unleashed. The rain was bad enough, but the flood is overwhelming. The old sayings, "When it rains, it pours" and "Trouble always comes in pairs," seem to hold true again and again. Some situations we face are like floods. Often orchestrated by the evil one, they are designed not only to take us down but also to take us out. We must remember that help is on the way. The Bible says, "When the enemy shall come in like a flood, the Spirit of the LORD shall lift up a standard against him" (Isaiah 59:19, KJV). A "standard" is a banner or national flag displayed on military ships and aircraft, often with the special insignia of a branch or unit of the armed forces. Do we have the standard of God flying on our house to defend us in times of trouble? Have we built our "house" for the Lord? Jesus said,

> Anyone who listens to my teaching and follows it is wise, like a person who builds a house on solid rock. Though the rain comes in torrents and the floodwaters rise and the winds beat against that house, it won't collapse because it is built on

bedrock. But anyone who hears my teaching and doesn't obey it is foolish, like a person who builds a house on sand. When the rains and floods come and the winds beat against that house, it will collapse with a mighty crash.
(Matthew 7:24-27, NLT)

Rain and storms come into the life of every human being. We can shelter under the umbrella of faith, knowing that such storms will fill and renew wells of water because God always brings something good out of every challenging situation (Romans 8:28, KJV). The same rain falls on everyone. There will be good times and bad times. If we have faith, however, we have some shelter from the storm.

We can raise a protective umbrella, knowing that we will get through the worst of the storm and see better days to come. The sun will come out for the believer.

TAKEAWAYS

- Good and bad things happen to everyone. "That ye may be the children of your Father which is in heaven: for He maketh His sun to rise on the evil and on the good, and sendeth rain on the just and on the unjust" (Matthew 5:45, KJV).
- While in the desert, do what you know to do. Do what you were trained to do. Like any good soldier, your training will kick in for your survival.
- During sunny times, we should be humble and generous with those who are less fortunate than we are.
- During rainy times, we need to raise the umbrella of faith as a covering from the storm. We know that such storms will fill and renew wells of water, because God always brings something good out of every challenging situation (Romans 8:28, KJV).

15
DIG YOUR OWN WELLS OR DIG YOUR OWN GRAVE: THE VALUE OF GIVING COOL CUPS OF WATER IN THE DESERT

If we are trying to live up to the words and instructions of our Lord Jesus Christ, we have built our house on a rock, no matter what storms may come. No matter how much we are battered and beaten, we will still stand. Our "houses" (ourselves, our marriages, and our families) will be safe, spiritually if not physically. Enduring to the end and hearing the Lord say, "Well done, good and faithful servant" is ultimately all that matters.

Of course, we are not only here for our loved ones and ourselves. We are here for the sake of others—to love others as we love ourselves and those dearest to us. Like offering a cold cup of water to others in the desert, giving others your time, money, and talents is a way to be sure your own wells never run dry.

What does it mean to choose between digging your own wells or digging your own grave? Digging wells means cultivating good relationships with other people. People are the world's greatest natural resource. If you know plenty of good people and they know you, and you have a relationship that involves a healthy circuit of giving and receiving, then you have "wells" that will help sustain you when the desert gets too dry.

In his book, *Dig Your Well Before You're Thirsty: The Only Networking Book You Will Ever Need*, Harvey Mackay says that an excellent network is important to success on every level. But a good network is not just a group of people to whom you turn in times of need. A great network is "the result of a lifetime of caring about people, of learning about them, spending time, and paying attention. It's the result of a lifetime of networking—that is, a lifetime of asking what you can do for someone else."[ix] Mackay points out that a real network means having people you can call at 2 a.m. in an emergency, knowing that they will come through for you. When you are in need, you have wells you can tap for water. Why? Because you took your friends' 2 a.m. calls and came through for them. You stayed in touch. You built relationships with them. You dug your wells before you got thirsty, and you nurtured those wells by giving other people cold cups of water when they were caught high and dry in the desert. Good relationships are as necessary as water.

"Network as if your life depended on it, because it does," Mackay counsels in chapter 16.[x] He recommends that everyone should at least have a way to contact a good doctor, a good lawyer, and a good accountant. These resources should not merely be people with letters after their names that designate their fields of expertise: M.D., Esq., and C.P.A. They should be professionals whom the people in your network highly recommend.

Knowing good people is like digging a well in a place where you know there is water. People are a tremendous source of information and support. Don't overlook this natural resource. At the same time, don't only build relationships to replenish your personal water supply. Be ready to hand out plenty of cool water yourself.

In his book *The Tipping Point*, Malcolm Gladwell also talks about the importance of networks. Good networks, he maintains, have changed history.[xi] Did you know, for example, that a second man rode out the same night as Paul Revere and delivered warnings that the British were coming? Do you know his name? Of course you don't. I don't either. That's because he wasn't a networker, and Paul Revere was. Paul Revere knew everybody who was anybody, and he knew everybody else too! A recent commercial shows Paul Revere using a cell phone to send the warning about the British, and then resuming a fireside game of charades. This depiction is fairly true to his character! Revere was social. He belonged to revolutionary committees and clubs. He was a great silversmith with many customers and contacts. He attended numerous meetings and events. He knew everyone. When Paul Revere served as a catalyst to information, the Internet alone probably could have competed with him. He was Facebook, Instagram, Kik, Twitter, and LinkedIn combined. Because of his social networking abilities, word spread like wildfire, American resistance was mobilized overnight, and the rest, as they say, is history.

Networks are important. Think of the useful information you've picked up during fellowship after church. Someone drops the name of a website that you later use to make a profit by doing something creative. Someone mentions that a certain company is hiring, and you utilize that information to get a new and better job. Someone tells you about the book, *Teach Your Child to Read in 100 Easy Lessons*. Someone tells you to have your young kids eat a couple of pieces of bread before bed to stop bedwetting, and it works. Someone invites you to a birthday party next week. Someone mentions that her young adult daughter expressed interest in your young adult son and wonders if your families could get together for a barbecue. Networking is a source of support, information, and enlightenment. It is an enriching experience that can make life better all around.

But how do you do it well? As Harvey Mackay said, good networking means thinking about others, caring about others, and connecting with others—and they will naturally do the same for you.

Don't network with selfish motivations. Treat networking and building relationships as something good in themselves. The results and fruits will come. You're planting the seeds, and, if you water them with love, you will draw a harvest. Give cold cups of water to those who are in the desert. A kind word, a bit of helpful advice, an invitation, the name of a good doctor—those are cold cups of water that you can give to your neighbors, friends, relatives, and fellows in Christ. With every cup you share, you form a network of caring that benefits everyone involved and will come back to benefit you too.

The Power of Giving Cups of Cool Water

Mark 9:41 says, "If anyone gives you even a cup of water because you belong to the Messiah, I tell you the truth, that person will surely be rewarded" (NLT). I have read this verse many times and am still amazed at its depth, beauty, and gravity. Unlike people who soon forget deeds done to help others, the Lord always remembers. He never says, "What have you done for me lately?" In fact, the Word of God assures us, "God is not unjust. He will not forget how hard you have worked for Him and how you have shown your love to Him by caring for other believers, as you still do" (Hebrews 6:10, NLT). Proverbs 11:25 says, "The generous will prosper; those who refresh others will themselves be refreshed" (NLT). Generosity will be rewarded: give a cup of water, and you will receive a cup of water in return, often when you most need it.

Do you only have to give cold cups of water to those in power or those whom you hope will benefit you in some way? Certainly not! Don't save your smiles, jokes, kind words, and compliments only for those who are better off than you are. Give them to the troubled people, the marginal people, the people everyone else overlooks. When you do this, you serve Christ Himself, and you will experience drinking from the well that never goes dry—the well of living water.

Rudyard Kipling, who wrote *The Jungle Book, The Man Who Would Be King*, and many other famous stories and poems, lived and worked at the turn of the nineteenth century. His significance as an author still shows in the fact that movies are made from his works years after his death.

Rudyard Kipling wrote a poem called *Gunga Din* about a "water boy." A British colonialist in the army, Kipling served in India. Gunga Din is about an Indian who helped the British troops by bringing water to the wounded men after a battle. "For Gawd's sake, get the water, Gunga Din!" cry the men, who are in pain in the hot Indian sun.

The British troops did not treat Gunga Din well. They looked down on "natives" and people of color. In fact, the narrator of the poem confesses that he physically abused Gunga Din only to realize that, because of his kindness in bringing water to the suffering, Gunga Din was a great person. "Though I've belted you and flayed you," says the narrator, "by the living God that made you, you're a better man than I am, Gunga Din."

For Kipling, who was a British colonialist at the height of the British Empire, this was a huge admission. He was the author of the famous line, "the white man's burden," which referred to people of color on this earth. For the famous author to later confess that a dark-skinned Indian was a better man than he was—all because Gunga Din offered water to those who suffered—represented a monumental shift in Kipling's thinking. Probably after experiencing an incident similar to the one in the poem, the influential writer wrote a confession about Gunga Din that made racism obsolete in the minds of anyone who read it.

This is the transforming power of cold cups of water. You never know when an act of kindness will change a perspective, change a life, or change someone's view of reality. A cold cup of water can truly change the world.

A Silent Witness

Many times, we believe that because we do not verbally share the gospel of Jesus Christ with others, we are not doing the Lord's work.

Even those who do not profess Christ as Lord and Savior verbally, however, can show the hand of God on their lives by the way they live in front of others every single day. This happens in the workplace, with neighbors, with store clerks at the coffee shop. They all see the way we live our lives. Many people have been converted by someone who gave silent witness through upright and kind living.

"What makes you the way you are?" people will ask. "What is behind you?" That is the perfect time to say, "It is my faith. I will tell you more, if you want to know." We earn the right to witness because of the life we live. This is why Jesus said for us to let our lights shine among men that they might see our good works and glorify the Father who is in Heaven (Matthew 5:16).

I remember the story of a Christian executive who worked for a large, multi-national automotive manufacturer based in Tehran, Iran, for five years. He worked with other executives as well. Due to his personal standards and ethic of hard work, he was the first one to arrive in the morning and the last one to leave in the evening. When extra or challenging work was proposed, he took it on. He did excellent work in addition to his willingness to take on more. It was also part of his personal standards and Christian ethics to present a smile and a positive, cheerful attitude at all times.

This man was personally frustrated that he could not talk about his faith in Jesus Christ. In fact, it is illegal to share about Jesus Christ in some Muslim countries, and Iran was no exception.

When it was time for him to finish his work there and depart for home, the Iranian president of the company took him aside and asked, "Can I talk to you?"

The businessman followed the Iranian executive to his office, fearful that perhaps he had done something wrong somehow. He tried to think of any possible negative feedback that might follow him back to the United States.

In private, the president of the Iranian company told him what a wonderful executive and manager he was. The president said this was not only his opinion; it was also the opinion of the other executives, his peers, and the people under this man's management. Other executives had been good, he said, but this man surpassed them all, and the president wanted to express his appreciation. What was more, the president wanted to know what caused this man to be the way he was.

The Christian executive asked if he could be candid, and the Iranian agreed. Then the American businessman shared about his relationship with Jesus Christ. Like a modern-day Daniel going into the lion's den, this Christian witnessed for the Lord in a land where it was illegal to do so. His life had earned him the right to witness even in a land inhospitable to his religion.

We earn the right to witness through the way we lead our lives. When you live out a silent witness, you are giving cold cups of water in the desert, and people know it and appreciate it. Often, they will want to know what motivates you to do so, and, at the very least, they will respect your faith even if they cannot yet come to share it.

Another example of a silent witness is the Amish. They are best known for living old-fashioned lives without cars and telephones in the heart of Pennsylvania Dutch (actually Deutsch, for German) country. They wear outdated clothes and do not have electricity in their homes. They live by nineteenth-century rural standards in order to keep their communities of faith close-knit. They are not anti-technology. They simply do not want the ringing of a telephone to interrupt a family's dinner or prayer time. They do not want the Internet or television, with their mixtures of good and evil, coming into their homes where they gather in family fellowship and prayer. Cars, they fear, would lead people to seek work and friends outside of their communities and eventually break up the colonies. They live this way out of a desire to focus on God, family, and one another in Christ within a community of faith.

Many Americans are charmed by the Amish. Handmade Amish woodcrafts and quilts are highly treasured. The Amish enjoy special congressional protection from certain laws. For example, they do not need to pay Social Security taxes because their families and communities provide a strong safety net for the elderly. When highway commissions proposed putting an interstate straight through Amish country, many people—not just the Amish—objected strenuously and got the project cancelled. This is part of the Amish's silent witness. People like and respect them whether or not they have ever spoken to an Amish person about faith.

The Amish have a saying about witnessing: "Preach—and if you must, speak." To them, actions speak louder than words when testifying to the presence of the Lord in their lives.

The Amish demonstrated an astonishing standard of Christian forgiveness to the world in 2005 when a deranged gunman entered one of their one-room country schoolhouses, shot five little girls dead, and wounded five others. Media from all over the world descended on humble Nickel Mines, Pennsylvania, where the ghastly murders had taken place. In some ways, those shots were heard around the world. It was a big scoop for reporters to speak about the carnage in the idyllic, bucolic, safe, and non-modern life of the Amish—a life that fills many Americans with nostalgia for a simpler, more natural, more faithful rural past. One author said that gunfire had invaded the last safe place in the American imagination.

Yet the media's narrative quickly shifted away from the bloodshed and horror when they encountered real Amish people. Reporters were shocked to find that the Amish were already in the process of forgiving the killer. Jaws dropped all over the world. The forgiving hearts of the Amish superseded the story about blood and gore in the schoolhouse. Forgiveness became the "scoop."

The Amish have a longstanding tradition of forgiveness because they believe that if they do not forgive others, they will not be forgiven. They believe that the merciful are blessed, for they will be shown mercy. To them, it was obvious that a Christian must forgive others, even if others shoot down your little daughters in cold blood. In fact, the Amish were astonished by the world's astonished reaction! "It's just simple Christianity, isn't it?" these good people asked the world.

The world stood back in amazement. *Christianity Today* voted the Amish to be the most inspiring Christians of the year. The story went from the sensationalism of the murders to a worldwide debate on what forgiveness is and how it can help heal wounds that seem impossible to salve in a troubled world.

The Amish lived up to their saying, "Preach—and if you must, speak." Few of them spoke to the media, but they showed by their actions what Christian forgiveness looks like. The Amish's forgiveness (which they did not advertise) included visiting the widow of the shooter, who had shot himself after committing the murders, and bringing food for her family. When millions of dollars poured into Amish country from sympathizers all over the world, the Amish asked if some of the funds could go to support the gunman's widow and children. Many Amish attended the gunman's funeral and sincerely prayed for him as he was buried. They did not believe he was an evil man. They believed he was a man who had performed evil actions, and that called for forgiveness.

"Preach—and if you must, speak." Our actions speak louder than our words.

Christians may show who they live and stand for by giving cold cups of water to a world that is a desert wasteland of pain, sorrow, suffering, and ignorance. Sometimes we do this by how we live. Other times, we must bravely speak for the Lord, even if it embarrasses us or makes us risk looking stupid. That is how we give cool cups of water in the desert too.

Recently, I had a tough week at work. To make matters worse, I missed a flight between consulting jobs. I had to fly through Las Vegas, and while waiting at the airport, a woman standing nearby caught my eye. The Lord whispered to me that she was a porn actress and that she needed my help.

Within minutes, she came to sit next to me. As she talked on her cell phone, I took out a business card and wrote on the back, "You are greatly beloved by Jesus," in the hopes of reaching her deepest heart and encouraging her to come to the well that never runs dry. When she finished her phone call, we struck up a conversation, and I asked her what she did for a living.

"I'm an actress," she said, confirming what the Lord had told me.

I gave her my business card and asked her not to read the back of it until she was on the plane, which she agreed to do. Then it was time to board. My seat was in the back, and hers was in the front, and I thought that was the end of the incident.

Yet, as I sat in the back of the plane, I felt that the Lord was not finished. I felt all sorts of things, including an impending fear that the woman would contract a disease—specifically, hepatitis—from activities she would engage in that weekend with people who meant her no good. I have read that pornography stars sometimes get diseases like HIV/AIDS right on the movie sets as they perform. I felt so much anguish for this woman. I felt that she had to run, or something truly terrible might happen. I felt an urgency to get her to the One who wanted her to have life and have it more abundantly—Jesus the Good Shepherd.

When the plane landed, I discovered that I had to go to a gate on a different concourse to catch the connecting flight. It was the last gate in a long concourse, a hike. I would have to sprint to make it, but when I got to a V in the concourse, the Lord told me, "You will wait."

I waited in quite a sweat, knowing that I would probably miss yet another plane. To my dismay, I also found that I had left my wallet on the last one! I would have to go all the way back and report it. I lamented to myself that it was probably already stolen.

Still, as I waited, I saw the woman walk toward me. In fact, she said, "Yes, Todd? What is it?" when she saw me. I told her I did not mean to come across as spiritually spooky, but I felt that the Lord had a warning to give her. I had written much of it down and put it in an envelope. I told her how much Jesus loved her and wanted to protect her. I poured out His anguish and concern for her. She thanked me, took my letter, and left.

I turned to start the long and stressful business of trying to trace my wallet. Suddenly, a flight attendant from the previous flight came up to me, out of breath from running the whole way. She had found my wallet, and she handed it to me.

If we let God use us as His instruments, even if we risk looking foolish by doing so, we will help God bring water in the desert and will live a well-watered life ourselves.

TAKEAWAYS

- Cultivating relationships with others means that we have resources to receive and to give.
- People are the world's greatest natural resource.
- Giving cold cups of water to others can change their lives for the better; it also replenishes our own spiritual nourishment.
- We can give cold cups of water without preaching out loud.
- Our lives should demonstrate our faith as much or more than our words do.
- We should not fear to give cold cups of water in the desert when the Lord directs us to. We may be saving a life.

16
JESUS: THE WELL, THE WATER, AND THE LIFE

Because of Isaac's obedience to God's will, the Lord fulfilled His promises to Isaac's descendants. God renewed His promise to Isaac through Jacob his son. Jacob's well became one that never ran dry, even centuries later. I once heard Jesse Duplantis say on a broadcast, "When you meet the conditions of the promise, you'll get the fulfillment of the promise." Jacob's well was like a symbol of the fulfilled promise of God to the descendants of Abraham, Isaac, and Jacob. Many nations would be blessed through their lineage, and their family would have an impact on the whole world.

Indeed, the fulfillment of that promise came to the well that Jacob himself dug when Jesus, the Lord and Savior, went there and acknowledged that it was originally dug by Jacob, the son of Isaac.

At the time Jesus visited Jacob's well, he was baptizing more disciples than John the Baptist (although it was Jesus' disciples who were baptizing, not Jesus Himself). Jesus left Judea and went back to Galilee. On the way, he had to go through Samaria. He passed through a town named Sychar, near a field that Jacob had given to his son Joseph. Jesus was treading on historical ground.

John 4:6 says, "Jacob's well was there; and Jesus, tired from the long walk, sat wearily beside the well about noontime" (NLT). A Samaritan woman came to draw water from the well, and Jesus asked her to please give Him a drink. "The woman was surprised, for Jews refuse to have anything to do with Samaritans. She said to Jesus, 'You are a Jew, and I am a Samaritan woman. Why are you asking me for a drink?'" (John 4:9, NLT)

Hatred between the Jews and the Samaritans extended well over 700 years before Christ, when most tribes of Israel were taken into captivity while the impoverished Jews were left behind. Instead of these poor Jews remaining faithful to the Mosaic and Levitical laws, they intermarried with the locals and embraced the worship of other gods in their homes—practices strictly forbidden. As a result, more faithful Jews considered the mixed-raced Samaritans to be accursed people. They were not allowed to sacrifice at the temple in Jerusalem. So, even in Jesus' day, hostility persisted between the Jews and the Samaritans. The Jews looked down on the Samaritans for not worshipping God in the "right" way.

When the Samaritan woman commented on the division between the Jews and Samaritans, Jesus replied, "If you only knew the gift God has for you and who you are speaking to, you would ask me, and I would give you living water" (John 4:10, NLT).

The woman was puzzled by this and took Jesus literally. She noted that he didn't have a rope or a bucket, and the well was deep. Besides, she thought Jesus was a little presumptuous: "Do you think you're greater than our ancestor Jacob, who gave us this well? How can you offer better water than he and his sons and his animals enjoyed?" (John 4:12, NLT).

Jesus replied, "Anyone who drinks this water will soon become thirsty again. But those who drink the water I give will never be thirsty again. It becomes a fresh, bubbling spring within them, giving them eternal life" (John 4:13, NLT).

Practical woman that she was, she said she wanted that kind of water so she wouldn't have to come back to the well over and over again. She was still thinking in earthly, fleshly terms when Jesus was trying to speak to her of spiritual truths. He asked her to go and call her husband and come back. When she said she had no husband, Jesus then told her some unflattering things about herself. He mentioned that she'd had several husbands and that the man she was living with was not her husband. He showed her that He knew about her sins without her having to verbalize them. That must have shocked her. At the same time, Jesus was kind to her. She didn't run away from Him, telling people how mean He was. She stayed and listened, spellbound, and told Him that He was a prophet.

Then something interesting happened. She started to talk about the division between the Jews and the Samaritans, and how her ancestors worshipped on the mountain but that the Jews contended that the faithful could only worship in the temple in Jerusalem. Jesus basically said that the place of worship didn't matter. Then He added, "The time is coming—indeed it's here now—when true worshipers will worship the Father in spirit and in truth. The Father is looking for those who will worship him that way. For God is Spirit, so those who worship Him must worship in spirit and in truth" (John 4:23-24, NLT).

In other words, Jesus directed the Samaritan woman back to the point of the encounter. She seemed receptive and mentioned the coming of the Messiah. Since the Samaritans believed in a future Messiah, the woman said that she knew the Messiah was coming. When he did, she was sure that he would explain everything to them. Then Jesus proclaimed, "I am the Messiah" (John 4:26, NLT).

She believed Him and finally left all ideas about earthly water behind, including her water jar (John 4:28, NLT). She headed into the town to tell everyone to "Come and see" (John 4:29, NLT). Jesus knew all about her, she explained to them, and she thought He might be the Christ. The woman was an instrument of conversion for many people that day. Based on her testimony, they went to see, hear, and decide for themselves whether or not Jesus was the Savior of the world (John 4:42, NLT).

In this biblical passage, Jesus does two things. He gives us a living model of the fact that God doesn't care about the particulars of where and how we worship—only that we worship in spirit and in truth. Jesus was just as anxious to reach the Samaritans as He was to reach the Jews. In fact, He was basically witnessing on His "lunch break" while the disciples went for food. Second, Jesus told the woman that if we try to use physical means to fill spiritual needs, our needs will remain long after the physical comforts are gone. There is only one place to go to quench our spiritual thirst: to the Lord Jesus Himself.

This point is underscored when Jesus' disciples returned to the well area with food and Jesus refused to eat. Just as He said that He had the water of eternal life, He now asserted to His disciples that He had food to eat that they knew nothing about (John 4:32). He went further and explained that for Him, real food was to do the work of the Father, and He compared all the people who were prepared to receive Him to a harvest (John 4:35).

How often do we turn to fleshly, worldly comforts rather than drinking from the well of eternal life? Park benches and city sidewalks are filled with people who have lost their ability to cope, turned to the bottle, and refused to come to terms with why they do what they do. Worse, they are seemingly unable to turn their lives around.

This is an extreme example, but consider "Joe" or "Joanna" Christian (or even yourself), who goes from relationship to relationship, longing to be wanted but never realizing that loneliness is a condition of the heart, not of the body. The Samaritan woman had had five "husbands" and was now involved with a lover. She is a prime example of someone who tried to fulfill spiritual needs with physical ones. She tried to comfort her heart by using the flesh, and Jesus corrected her and finally got her to think about the true source of comfort and love: God.

You may hunger and thirst for love. We all do. But if you try to fulfill that thirst with person after person, one misdirected relationship after another, you will experience an unimaginable desert of love in your life. Instead of filling up the reservoirs of love in your heart, you will deplete them, making yourself less capable of sustaining a true, long-term love relationship with someone. Your well of love will be empty when someone worthy of your love comes along. You will have nothing to give because you drank too much from the waters that do not give life and avoided the waters that do.

It is interesting that Jesus met a woman at the well who was particularly challenged in the area of relationships with the opposite sex. This ancient story seems more relevant than ever in our day, when many movies, songs, and TV shows glorify sexuality. Often, it seems that we worship the idol of the body and its beauty. Talk shows, comedians' presentations, and sitcoms are full of sexual jokes, implying that everyone is having sex all the time and that sex is the ultimate goal of human existence. Has there ever been an era as strongly worshipful of human sexuality as our era?

Certainly, no other era in history had the electronic means to convey sexual images. A few decades ago, a person had to sneak ashamedly into an out-of-the-way shop or store aisle to purchase magazines full of sexual images. Now, these are available at the touch of a computer button in the privacy and solitude of one's own home. In fact, they sometimes pop up unasked for.

Jesus' message to the woman at the well was never more relevant than it is to our society today. His voice echoes down the ages, telling us to stop thinking so much about the body and about the comforts of the flesh. Jesus enjoins us to focus on the life of the soul. We need to invite the indwelling of the Holy Spirit so that we can have a different kind of life, full of life-giving bread and water, food and drink for our souls.

Jesus enjoins us to come to the well of living water, to cleanse ourselves, and to fill our hearts with his love. That is a surer path to true romantic love than clinging to the body of the first human being who will have you. Some people cling to another person whether he or she is abusive, uses drugs, is alcoholic, expects the partner to do all the work, or is sexually unfaithful. Anyone like that is an empty well. You will never satisfy your thirst that way. Even concentrating on fleshly love with people who are trying to be loving and good—even if they are fellow believers—cannot satisfy the thirst of the soul. Only Jesus and the Holy Spirit can quench that thirst.

This is not to say that the flesh is bad. It needs water, food, clothing, shelter, healthcare, transportation, and sexual expression. But it is essential that we give the body those things at the right time, in the right way, with the proper motivation, with the proper person, and in the will of God. The love of Jesus should come first. Then all other things will fall into place; all other things will follow in their proper order (Matthew 6:33).

Try to recall times when you were surrounded by people you knew and still felt alone. You can be in a room packed with bodies and yet feel like a stranger. During those times, remind yourself of Christ's promises:

- Hebrews 13:5: "For He Himself has said, "I will never leave you nor forsake you" (NLT).

- John 16:33: "I have told you all this so that you may have peace in me. Here on earth you will have many trials and sorrows. But take heart, because I have overcome the world" (NLT).

- John 14:23: "All who love me will do what I say. My Father will love them, and we will come and make our home with each of them" (NLT).

- John 4:14: "But those who drink the water I give will never be thirsty again. It becomes a fresh, bubbling spring within them, giving them eternal life" (NLT).

In John 7:38, Jesus again compares Himself to a well: "Anyone who believes in me may come and drink! For the Scriptures declare, 'Rivers of living water will flow from his heart'" (NLT). In other words, as John points out, the Spirit will flow from within that person. The person will be filled with the Holy Spirit, which flows like a river of life from the heart.

Christ, knowing the history of the well, uses the analogy of Jacob's well to describe the principle of eternal life to the Samaritan woman and to turn her mind away from fleshly comforts. He wants her to recognize and seek the deepest comfort for the yearning of the human heart: the yearning for God.

Proverbs 14:26-27 says, "Those who fear the LORD are secure; he will be a refuge for their children. Fear of the LORD is a life-giving fountain; it offers escape from the snares of death" (NLT).

Is something clogging the flow of living water in your life? Are you having doubts about whether the Lord is working in your life?

Are you engaging in practices that block the flow of water and choke off the supply? Have you filled your own wells with sand, dust, and dirt?

Jesus said that every hair on our heads is numbered (Luke 12:7). God knows what we do to choke off our supply of water and contaminate our inner wells of life. We may try to hide from ourselves, but we can't hide from God. The Lord knows. Jesus knew everything there was to know about the woman at the well. Every idle word and deed shall be accounted for. Every person shall be judged, and every knee shall bow. And yet God desires that none perish and that all come to everlasting life. It's time to get rid of the clogs and the dirt thrown down our wells; it's time to allow God to bring forth living waters to others and to ourselves.

If we know the Lord and make Him known, we are able to live an abundant life of passion, purpose, and destiny. As we seek His face daily for guidance and strength, we begin to resemble Him more and more. It's natural for others to want to know what makes us so fulfilled. Our relationships at home and at work and with neighbors will be sweetened and seasoned with grace as we love one another with God's love. As we give our money, time, and talents to help others, we make way for a flow of the living water that will help us and everyone around us to live more abundantly. Then, we will drink from the well that will never run dry, because it is supplied by the Source that is Jesus.

TAKEAWAYS

- Jesus wants us to concentrate on things of the Spirit, not of the flesh.

- God knows all about us and the fleshly ways we use to try to comfort ourselves, just like He knew about the woman at the well.

- God the Comforter has comfort that cannot compare to the comforts of the flesh.

- Jesus is the source of living water—the only well that leads to eternal life.

- "When you meet the conditions of the promise, you'll get the fulfillment of the promise" (Dr. Jesse Duplantis).

17
START DIGGING

What have we learned from the example of Isaac, the son of Abraham and the father of Jacob—one of the most significant figures in biblical history? Let's revisit some key points.

- Embrace change. Change is the only constant in life. Change will come. Changing for the better is good. If God asks you to change your life (even to travel to a land not your own where you will be a foreigner like Isaac), be wise enough to follow God's lead.

- Stop (be still), Look (seek God), and Listen (receive godly guidance). Going through life without God's guidance is like being a drunken man on a slippery floor. Learn to listen to the voice of God. Train your ears to hear the Lord's voice by reading the Word of God aloud. Faith and direction come from hearing, listening, and then taking action. When Isaac had problems, he usually took them to God in prayer.

- Move out (take action). Actions speak louder than words and are an important part of witnessing. Isaac often moved everything he had when it seemed right to do so.

• "Everything comes to him who hustles while he waits" (Thomas Edison). Isaac didn't sit around while he was in the foreign land. He worked hard to build up his herds and flocks. He became a wealthy man because God blessed his efforts.

• Adapt to change, but don't compromise godly standards in order to "go with the flow" of change. In other words, don't go against God's will just because you are afraid for your own safety.

• Make your spouse and family a priority.

• Let life's disappointments drive you to your knees to move closer to Christ instead of further away. When Isaac learned that his wife Rebekah was barren, he turned to the Lord instead of wallowing in his disappointment.

• Learn to begin again by wiping the slate clean so that you can be a finer tuning fork for God. Rather than further stirring up trouble, Isaac was accommodating when his wealth made the Philistines jealous. He moved on again and again.

• Expect difficult times. Times like these give God an opportunity to show you how wonderful He is, more than you ever imagined, because your weakness is His strength.

- Use the desert times as training and testing times. Martin Luther King, Jr., said, "The content of a man's character is not where he stands in times of comfort and convenience, but where he stands at times of challenge and controversy."

- Digging the well doesn't mean getting to keep all the water. Offer cold cups of water to others.

- When in the valley, dig your own wells instead of your own grave. Cultivate relationships with others.

- Peace with your enemies is always possible when God is your negotiator. Isaac won over his enemies by being a good and accommodating man in whom they could see God.

- Learn to own nothing and possess everything. It helps to travel light when you are going through the desert in a foreign land.

- Realize that the truth will always outlive a lie. If God has given you power, then the seat of power is where you sit, no matter what the world says. Isaac went to Gerar as a stranger fleeing a desert depression, and he left an honored and wealthy man.

- Realize that secular work is full-time service. Isaac didn't neglect his flocks and herds to witness to the Philistines and Abimelech. Instead, he went about his business in a godly way, and it became clear to them that God was with him.

- Realize that the person who serves will never go without. As the Bible says, the water of a generous person will be sure.

- Pray. Pray again. Keep praying until your answer comes.

- Don't just ask for material items or specific outcomes. Ask for strength, forgiveness, love, deliverance from evil and sin, and the ability to navigate your way through the desert. Ask for more love and insight on someone with whom you're in conflict. Ask why things haven't panned out in a godly way yet, and learn what you can do about it.

- Ask for the favor of God in all your endeavors, large and small.

- Live to live again. Life on this earth is but preparation for eternity. Store up your treasures in Heaven, not on earth. Search for the living water from the well of eternal life, the well symbolized by the well that Jacob, Isaac's son, dug.

- Remember that he who believes in Christ never dies.

- Do what you know to do. Many people are looking for a word from the Lord when they have not yet done the most recent thing the Lord commanded them to do.

- Clean out your well! "Whatever's in the well will show up in the bucket" (unknown). Isaac wasn't too proud to re-dig his father's wells.

- Don't wallow in self-pity. Learn to encourage yourself in God. Gratitude is the antidote to self-pity. Do you have too much work to do? Be thankful that you have work!

- Prayer is action. The reason the miraculous is not occurring is because we have not paved the way for God to move through prayer.

- Prayer changes you first because you introduce God into the problem, and He loves that. The Heavenly Father takes great delight in helping His children.

- Reach out to those around you. Stop living selfish lives. There is plenty of work to do, and there are plenty of people with whom to share the love of Christ. Start in your home, and then change your neighborhood.

- Always remember your assets—your family. The world says that if you don't like your family situation, divorce yourself from it. God never divorces us, no matter what we do.

- Look for the log in your own eye before you decide to take the splinter out of your spouse's or children's eyes.

- Keep plowing, sowing seeds, and watering, but leave it to God to bring about the increase.

- Remember who your enemy *really* is (hint: it's not your spouse, friend, coworker, or boss), and wage warfare in prayer. Satan has committed acts of war that cause havoc in your home, on the job, and in the church. He tries to plug the "wells" on which you have spent your blood, sweat, and tears. He's working to steal your joy and wear you out. Serve the enemy an eviction notice through prayer! The Word of God says, "Resist the devil and he shall flee from you" (James 4:7). And while he is beating a hasty retreat, take back what he stole from you.

- Stop flirting with secret sin. Confess it and forsake it. God knows about it. You're not fooling Him, any more than Jesus was fooled by the woman at the well when she said she had no husband.

- "There's a high cost to low living." (Dr. Edwin Louis Cole)

- "The best throw of the dice is to throw them away" (English proverb).

- Ensure your happiness, life, love, and wealth by living an upright life in God. Like Isaac, you will be blessed.

- Stop being jealous of the others. As Isaac knew, there is "Plenty of Room" for all.

- Delayed obedience becomes disobedience. What if Isaac had waited to go to Gerar? There would have been no story, no land, no descendants, no wells, and no Israel as a landing platform for the Messiah.

- God has got your back: He is in front, in back, underneath, above, on the left, and on the right, and He's living inside you. "For I hold you by your right hand—I, the LORD your God. And I say to you, 'Don't be afraid. I am here to help you'" (Isaiah 41:13, NLT). When Isaac was uneasy, the Lord appeared to him, reassured him, and helped him. He is ready to reassure and help you too.

- Your success in life is measured by your obedience to God.

- God may interrupt your life. ("Go to Gerar. Now leave Gerar.")

- "Love everybody but move with the movers."
  – Pastor Rick Warren

- God explains the terms of His covenant. He renewed His promise to Isaac, even though Isaac, as a son of Abraham, already knew about it. God also reaffirmed to Jacob that the same blessing of multiple descendants, land, and influence would be passed down to their family from generation to generation.

- God commands us to decide and take action. Invitations are optional; commands are not.

- The Holy Spirit of God is not dormant. He is at work in the earth, bringing about God's eternal purpose and driving the world closer every day to the imminent return of the Lord Jesus Christ. When Jesus stayed by Jacob's well and talked to the woman, He promised that he was a well of living water, bubbling up to eternal life. Jesus is the culmination of the promises made to Abraham, Isaac, and Jacob. Throughout the ages since, the Holy Spirit has come as living water to the spirits of men and women, preparing us to receive the Lord when he comes again.

18

CONCLUSION: PARTING THOUGHTS

Are we Christians too busy looking at our glass of water as half empty rather than half full? I think so. Since we have so many gifts from God, why aren't more Christians rejoicing? If we were sending out signals of joy and fulfillment, wouldn't that be a better witness to our world? Maybe we aren't drinking at the well enough to fill our hearts with life-giving waters.

Still, no one ever said that the Christian life was easy. We may be pressed down, but we are not crushed. We may be confused, but we are not in despair. We may be struck down, but we are not destroyed (2 Corinthians 4:8-9). The Word of God says, "When people's lives please the LORD, even their enemies are at peace with them" (Proverbs 16:7, NLT).

Is your life a wellspring of love, peace, and joy? If not, why not? Is it because you think you don't have enough time, money, energy, talent, et cetera? If you are experiencing a desert time where there isn't enough of some of those things, then it's time to dig a well, build a prayer altar, pray and worship the Lord. Start sharing cups of cold water from your well. Then your own cup will overflow. Luke 6:38 says, "Give, and you will receive. Your gift will return to you in full—pressed down, shaken together to make room for more, running over, and poured into your lap. The amount you give will determine the amount you get back" (NLT). If you give to others, you will be given a more-than-full amount in return.

Keep your well clean and dug out. Defend your well from attacks of the enemy. Guard your heart and mind by replenishing with prayer, fasting, studying the Word of God, praise, worship, and bringing every thought in alignment with Jesus Christ and godly actions. Again, share cold cups of water with others who are suffering. But don't neglect to drink a cup of water yourself.[

Jeremiah 17:5-8 (NLT) says it best. The prophet enjoins us not to trust in "mere humans" or to "rely on human strength," else we will be "like stunted shrubs in the desert, with no hope for the future." We will have to "live in the barren wilderness, in an uninhabited salty land." We are not to live according to the ways of the world or the ways of the flesh. The Bible says this again and again.

"But blessed are those," Jeremiah goes on to say (verses 7-8), "who trust in the LORD and have made the LORD their trust and confidence. They are like trees planted along a riverbank, with roots that reach deep into the water. Such trees are not bothered by the heat or worried by long months of drought. Their leaves stay green, and they never stop producing fruit."

The purpose of your desert experience is to grow (mature) in the faith. We overcome by the blood of the Lamb and by our testimony (Revelation 12:11). But, like Paul, we must be able to say, "for I have learned, in whatsoever state I am, therewith to be content"

(Philippians 4:11, KJV). Reclaim the old wells; find and establish new wells to be refreshed. Be like a tree planted by the living water, having no fear of the heat by day, the cold by night, and the sand all around you. Find your oasis in the desert, and rest. God will lead you out of your desert experience victoriously. On your journey out, however, know that *you* have changed. The desert is still the same. You have learned to survive in a barren and dry place. Then and only then will you never cease or fail to bear fruit.

You will live "The Well-Watered Life."

ABOUT THE AUTHOR

Todd L. Shuler is an internationally known management consultant, speaker, ordained minister, and author of four books.

He brings a background of management consulting and business and IT Strategy and Implementation for both the private and public sectors, having worked for Deloitte and Ernst & Young. He also previously worked for On Assignment, Citizant, Texas Instruments, and Bank of America.

Todd graduated from the Terry College of Business at the University of Georgia with a Bachelor of Business Administration in Management Information Systems and a minor in Japanese Language and Literature. He is currently pursuing his Master of Divinity at Reformed Theological Seminary as well as his Master of Business Administration (MBA) at the J. Whitney Bunting School of Business at Georgia College and State University.

Todd is passionate about discovering the Will of God for his life as well as connecting people to God, to their purpose, and to others. He and his wife Evetta have three wonderful children.

UPCOMING BOOKS BY TODD SHULER

One Month of The Well-Watered Life Devotional
ISBN-978-0-9889589-2-0

Dive headfirst into this perfect companion devotional to *The Well-Watered Life* by inspirational author, Todd Shuler. Allow this book to guide you in experiencing God's peace in new and profound ways as you spend 31 days of resting in His Presence.

The Tiger Tamer
ISBN-978-0-9889589-1-3

Take your Business from the Wilderness to the Center Ring

Business can feel like a jungle out there! But successful business management pro Todd Shuler has come to tame the tigers and teach you how. Using a clever allegory of taming a tiger—your business—Todd Shuler gives you the "Greatest Know on Earth" when it comes to being business savvy under the Big Top—or within your walls.

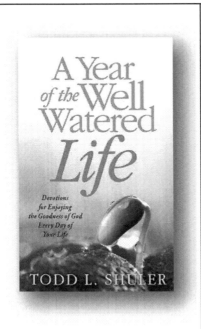

**A Year of
the Well-Watered Life**

ISBN-978-0-9889589-3-7

One Month of Resting in God's Presence not long enough for you? We couldn't agree more. *A Year of the Well-Watered Life* gives you biblically based devotions for enjoying God's goodness through every season of your life.

As the old Christian expression goes, "Every day with Jesus is sweeter than the day before." Get this Holy Spirit-inspired devotional and experience the living Christ in new and exciting ways.

---

[i] John Maxwell, *Failing Forward* (Nashville: Thomas Nelson, 2000) 13.

[ii] Jack Hayford, *Pursuing the Will of God: Reflections and Meditations on the Life of Abraham* (Sisters OR: Multnomah Publishers, Inc., 1997) 42.

[iii] Kirbyjon Caldwell, *The Gospel of Good Success* (New York: Fireside [Simon & Schuster], 1999).

[iv] Debbie Macomber, *Mrs. Miracle* (New York: HarperPaperbacks, 1996).

[v] C. S. Lewis, *Mere Christianity* (New York: HarperOne Reprint Edition, 2012) 124–25.

[vi] Stormie Omartian, *The Power of a Praying Wife* (Eugene OR: Harvest House, 1997).

[vii] Mary Pipher, *The Shelter of Each Other: Rebuilding Our Families* (New York: G. P. Putnam's Sons, 1996).

[viii] Jack Hayford, *Pursuing the Will of God: Reflections and Meditations on the Life of Abraham* (Sisters OR: Multnomah, 1997).

[ix] Harvey Mackay, *Dig Your Well Before You're Thirsty: The Only Networking Book You Will Ever Need* (New York: CurrencyBook, published by Doubleday, a division of Random House, 1997) 2.

[x] Ibid., 86.

[xi] Malcolm Gladwell, *The Tipping Point: How Little Things Can Make a Big Difference* (Boston: Back Bay Books, 2002).

Made in the USA
Lexington, KY
23 February 2014